YALE COLLEGE:

SOME THOUGHTS RESPECTING ITS FUTURE.

A SERIES OF ARTICLES,

BY

TIMOTHY DWIGHT,

PROFESSOR IN THE THEOLOGICAL DEPARTMENT.

NEW HAVEN:
PRINTED BY TUTTLE, MOREHOUSE AND TAYLOR.
1871.

The Articles, which are here brought together, were originally printed in the New Englander—in the numbers of that Quarterly which appeared in July and October, 1870, and in April, July, and October, 1871. The author, as he now presents them in a collected form to the graduates and friends of Yale College, indulges the hope that they may be of some small service in the way of awakening large and comprehensive views of what the institution needs, and, thus, of promoting the growth of a true University in New Haven. One or two of the suggestions presented in the opening Articles have been adopted within the last six months, (in particular, certain initiatory steps have been taken with reference to a more perfect organization of some of the courses of study in the Philosophical Department,) but the author has deemed it not improper to leave them in their original form, begging the reader to notice the date of their first publication, and to bear in mind their importance as connected with the wisest and most comprehensive plans for the future. He would only add the expression of his confidence that the recently developed enthusiasm of the graduates, in connection with the matter of the Woolsey Fund, will incline them to pardon any repetition, which they may notice, in his earnest appeal to the College authorities to enter upon the work of providing for its most vital present want—the want of greater pecuniary endowments.

YALE COLLEGE,
Nov. 10, 1871

YALE COLLEGE:

SOME THOUGHTS RESPECTING ITS FUTURE.

FIRST ARTICLE.

There is a somewhat general feeling, we believe, among those who are most deeply interested in Yale College, that the institution is about entering on a new era of its existence. The work of the last seventy years, it is felt, has been a good and a great one, but it is mainly accomplished. Like that of the first century of the College history, and like that of every epoch in the progress of every growing institution, it has laid the foundation for what is larger and higher than itself—not higher, indeed, in the nobleness of the working, but in that the working is nearer to the final and full completion of the plan. The past now is to open itself toward and into the future, and a great step forward is to be or ought to be taken. Indications of this are seen on every side. The suggestions which are presented by those who think earnestly upon the subject of education; the criticisms of the College which, for some reason or other, have been so frequent of late and which, we regret to say, have not been always made either in a wise or a generous spirit; the proposition to change the governing board of the institution by the introduction of new members from the alumni; and the sentiments and aspirations of the instructors within the College walls, all alike bear witness that the coming years are looked upon as containing within themselves possibilities and hopes, which as yet have been unrealized. What are to be the characteristic features of the new era, and what its peculiar and distinctive work, are, therefore, questions of much importance, at the present time, and worthy of serious consideration. Our object is to present, in a series of Articles, some thoughts in answer to these questions.

The first and most important work to be done in the years immediately before us is, as we believe, a work of *unification.* Yale College, like most of the older American Colleges, began as a sort of high school. It carried forward the education of the young men who came to it beyond the point which they had reached in the lower schools of the time, and opened the way for them to enter upon their active life. But it was limited in its aims, and in the results which it accomplished, by the limitations of the age. Men had not come, as yet, to take the widest views of education. The various sciences and branches of learning had scarcely begun to develop themselves—some of them had not begun to exist. Even in the department of theological science, which was nearest to the minds of the fathers, the demands and possibilities were comparatively small. A general course, moving on but a little way, was all which, as it would seem, could be devised. The wisdom of the early founders was displayed, not in their accomplishment of the entire work, but in the fact that the plan which they formed was one which would, readily and naturally, enlarge itself to meet every requirement or change of the future, so soon as the demand should arise. The school, which they established, would become a university in the course of generations. The College, which, in their day, was a whole in itself, would gradually become but one among several portions of a greater institution. It would lose something of its own prominence as it associated with itself other departments for more special training, but it would gain a new honor in their company, which it could never know without them. It was after the beginning of the present century that the change came. The new features of the times, and the growth to which we have alluded in all branches of knowledge, gave the opportunity, and, in giving the opportunity, they presented the call for a new work. The sagacious and far-seeing mind of the remarkable man, who, at that period, had the interests of the College in his special keeping, understood the call. He saw that, if the institution lingered in the old work, it might increase, indeed, in numbers and in influence, but it could never take the high place which was offered to it among the educational institutions of the country. Professional schools must be established, which should receive the students at their graduation from the collegiate or academic department, and fit them, by a special course of study, for their own peculiar sphere in the world. The beginning, at least, must be made, which should prepare the way for future growth and render possible the completion of the work. Accordingly, at the earliest practicable moment, he established one of these schools, and devised the plan for another, which was founded a few years later His immediate successors, who had been largely under his influence, carried forward the same plans. All the professional departments of the College were established, or strengthened, until some of them attained a considerable eminence. Finally, within the past twenty-five years, the Scientific School and the department of Philosophy and Philology have made the institution complete in its parts. The work of which we have thus briefly spoken, together with the advancement of scholarship in every branch of learning within the College, has been the work of the past half-century. We have alluded to it, however, not for its own sake, but because we would call attention to a point which is of especial importance. The history of these two great periods of the past shows that the development in this, as in other similar institutions in our country, has not been a development of all the parts together. It has been, on the contrary, a growth for a hundred years of one department alone by itself, and then an addition to this one department of others, which, from their later origin, have seemed to be gathered around it as their center. The life and vigor of our American Colleges—even where they have widened into Universities, as at Yale and Harvard—have continued largely at this center; and the governing powers have regarded the academical department as the object of their peculiar and almost their sole care. The institutions have thus, with all their enlargement and success, been, after all, rather colleges with certain outside sections than universities made up of coördinate and coequal branches. They have not had a well-rounded and perfect development, but one which has been partial and one-sided in its character. This result has been a natural, perhaps in some measure a necessary, result of the origin and history of the institutions. But of the reality of the fact we think no intelligent observer can doubt.

Now the point, which we have to urge, is, that the future years must unite these departments into a common whole, giving the same care to the growth of all. The age of mere colleges in this country, in a certain sense, is past. Not that colleges will not continue to exist, and to be needed, and to do a good work. But they are not to be the highest institutions to which we look forward, and which we shall ask for hereafter. The great centers of education, like Yale and Harvard, must be centers of universal education; and, if they cease to be so, they will sink to the level of a lower class of seminaries, which make no such claims as they are making. It needs no argument to prove this. The very peculiarity, which distinguishes these higher institutions as a class by themselves, is not the superiority of their instruction for undergraduate academical students or their superiority in respect to the number of their undergraduates. If these things be all which they have to elevate them, they will only reach the higher places among the institutions which have merely an academical course. They will be far in advance, indeed, of the colleges just established in the new states, but they will still belong in their company. If they are to leave their company altogether, they need something more than this. To the university—in the sense in which the word is most appropriately used, that is, as distinguished from the college—what have sometimes been called the "outside" schools are essential. They are, even, *the essential thing.* It will scarcely require any more argument to show, that, if these "outside" schools are to hold their proper place and to maintain a steady and permanent growth, this name, which has been assigned to them because their origin was later than that of the collegiate branch and they were thus added to it, must be laid aside as no longer suited to mark their real position. They must, in a word, become "inside" schools, having each and all of them the same rights and privileges and care with the original academic section of the university. If they do not have this, they cannot prosper in the long run. If they are left to provide for themselves altogether—in the expressive phrase of recent years, "hanging on the verge of the government"—they may succeed, for a while, through the power and self-devotion of the members of their faculties, but, when these men are called away or die, the institutions will prove to have little or no independent life of their own. They will show that they have rested on the reputation of individuals, and that the want of constant and watchful care from the central power has been fatal to them. We hold it to be even self-evident, that, if the governing body of any institution or of any country give their thoughts to one part of it alone, or if they manifestly place one part in their thoughts above the others, these other portions will, sooner or later, suffer in their life in consequence. Neglect, if it be only partial, always checks and dwarfs the thing neglected. If it be total, it destroys it—not, perhaps, as speedily, but almost as surely as does a violent putting it out of existence. If the medical school of a university, for example, is looked upon as of little consequence, because its number of students is smaller than that of the undergraduate or some other department, or because it is very limited in its funds and it seems a difficult matter to increase them, or because medical science, for the time, is regarded with less favor than physical or theological science, or for any other reason, it will, after a few years at the latest, lose something of its vital energy. It will gradually move towards the level at which others would place it, and, if it finally falls even below that level, it need, surely, be no matter of surprise. The feeling must be—if success is to be attained—a widely different one from this. The spirit of the University must be the spirit of unity and fraternity. If one member suffers, the sentiment must be that all the members, of necessity, suffer with it, and if one member rejoices, that all the members rejoice with it. So far from leaving those that are weaker or younger to move on as best they can, these more needy portions must have so much the greater encouragement and aid. This is the rule in every other institution or body in the world, and the necessity of its observance in these great educational institutions requires only to be stated, in order to be admitted by every candid mind. It is a rule which, if it be not observed, will show, by the results of its violation, how essential and fundamental it is. The whole body, in the course of time, will suffer, if any part of it is disregarded. It will inevitably lose the fullness of its glory. It will meet the penalty of its own neglect. The history of our larger institutions, in the past even, has proved the truth of what we say, in greater or less degree. If the future should be like the past, the coming history will prove it far more clearly. It will do so, because the past has been only the time of the beginning—of the arrangement and formation of the plan, so far as the more recent departments are concerned; but the future is to be the time of their progress and development—the time when the question of their permanent success, and, in connection with *their* success, of the success of *the University* is to be determined.

But how, it may be asked, is the unifying work, of which we have spoken, to be accomplished? If the result is demanded, what are the steps which must be taken in order to reach it? We answer, *in the first place,* that the general sentiment and feeling in the University must be in this direction, as we have already intimated. The old ideas, which have been the natural growth of the way and order in which the departments have come into existence, must pass away altogether, and in their place must arise the better and more correct views, which look upon the institution as made up of equal and equally important parts. Age or numbers, in this matter, must not be regarded as, necessarily, having any weight whatever. The branch of the university which was founded twenty-five years ago must be considered as important to the completeness of the whole body as that whose origin was more than a century earlier. And while the success of any school is to be determined, in a measure, by the number of its students, it must not be forgotten, that a law school of sixty or a hundred, or a department of philosophy or philology containing even twenty or thirty, may be as successful as an academical department of five hundred or a thousand. We say as successful, because it as nearly reaches the present possibilities of its growth. But supposing any section of the university not to be successful, as measured by this standard, or to be beginning to lose ground, it must gather to itself so much more of the energy of the governing power and of the sympathy of the whole body, and thus it must be borne up and carried forward to a new life. We believe that every officer of a great institution, like Yale, should be as ready to give or to labor for the prosperity of every other department of it—so far as the calls of his special work will allow—as for the one with which he is more particularly connected; and that every trustee or overseer should be equally and large-heartedly devoted to them all. There may be some apology if this has not always been the case in earlier times, but there will be none in the new era. It will be an abandonment of the work of the new era, at its very beginning, if these sentiments and feelings are wanting. But we rejoice to believe that they will not be wanting. There are unmistakable signs that these ideas are gaining ground in Yale College—whatever may be true of other colleges—and that the future is to see the completion of the plan here, which the past has only formed in its parts—the rounding out and perfecting of the University as a whole.

To the end of strengthening the sentiment to which allusion has been made, and as a further means of accomplishing the object in view, we think, *secondly*, that there should be not infrequent meetings of the several faculties of the university as one body, for consultation respecting the common interests. There are, in every such large educational institution, many questions continually arising, which have exclusive reference to particular departments. These should be reserved for the consideration and decision of the particular faculty of the department to which they belong. But there are, on the other hand, subjects of great importance, which pertain to the welfare of all alike, and to the advancement of the entire institution. Subjects of this nature, certainly, should not be limited to the deliberation of one or two of the separate faculties, but should be discussed in a general meeting. The interests of all should be fairly and fully represented, and the needs and claims of each should be urged, as they only can be, properly, by those who have the most intimate knowledge of them. The reasonableness and wisdom of such a course would seem to be evident at its very first suggestion. And yet, so strong has been the influence of the past history of our colleges an of the order of their development, that, as far as we a: aware, such common meetings have never, as yet, been know anywhere. In the future, we anticipate that they will b known, and, so soon as they are, it will be a matter of wond that they had not been held long before. Of the effect of suc meetings on the harmony and good feeling of the faculti towards each other, there can be no doubt. The opposi course, by which decisions affecting the general well-being a made by a part only of those interested, seems really a sort interference with privileges, much as if one of the faculti should attempt to control the affairs which are properly und the supervision of another. Wherever there is such interfe ence or want of kindly consideration, there can scarcely fai at times, to be a greater or less sense of a sort of injustice an a weakening, in some degree, of the ties that bind all togethe But when every one has free opportunity to say and to do a that he can for the common benefit—to make suggestions, an urge needed improvements, and meet all others in friendl discussion, and influence them, or be influenced by them—h will be, almost of necessity, a hearty well-wisher and helpe to his associates. Whether he chances to be in the minority or i the majority, he will be equally ready to aid in carrying ou the decision, or, at least, will feel that his views have receive respectful attention, and will, thus, be so far satisfied. The uni versity and the collegiate department of it—it cannot be to often repeated—are not the same thing. And, in the matter which have reference to the university, the members of th several faculties of the university should be consulted, just a truly as, in those which bear upon the collegiate departmen only, the discussion should be open to all the members of it particular faculty and not be limited to a selected portion o them. It must be so, as we believe, if the harmony of th faculties is to be always unbroken. It must be so, also, if th highest good of the institution is to be attained. The member of one faculty are, almost necessarily, limited in their view and sympathies to some extent. Men look upon subjects from their own standpoint, and they need to be influenced and mod ified in their opinions by the sentiments of those who have different position—or the common welfare will often be lost sight of. The officers whose daily work and thoughts are within the sphere of a theological department may feel as kindly as possible towards those belonging to the associated scientific school, but they cannot determine *alone* what is best for the two schools together. The two bodies need to confer freely with each other—the two sides need to be fully represented—in order to reach the most enlightened and liberal decision. The same thing is true of any other two departments, and even more true, if possible, of any one as related to all the rest.

And here, lest we may be misunderstood as giving to the faculties the power which belongs to the trustees or corporation, let us say that we have no such intention. The spheres of the two bodies are distinct, and the final controlling power is with the trustees. But we believe that all persons who have been familiar with our colleges or universities will agree with us in holding, that a very large proportion of the measures which are adopted by the trustees must originate with the faculties. The members of the corporation are generally non-resident. In many matters they cannot watch the progress and wants of the institution from day to day. They must look to the members of the board of instructors, oftentimes, for information and advice. If they attempt to go forward alone, mistakes of a very serious nature will, inevitably, be made. The faculties and the trustees should be in reality, if not in name, two houses in the government, and many measures should have their beginning only in the lower house. A college can be governed to death, as well as any other organization, and one of the dangers, to say the least, which is incidental to that change in the corporation, which meets so much favor at present, is that it will bring more interference from the higher powers with the freedom of the working of the University. This freedom has been the glory of Yale College in the past—even beyond all other colleges. We have heard the present President of Harvard University speak of it as one of the inestimable privileges of this institution, as compared with his own. The traditions and influences here are all in favor of it. The success and harmony of the college have depended more upon this, perhaps, than upon any other single cause. We hope the day may be far distant when it shall be lost in any measure. The ideal way, beyond all doubt, is that of a wise and hearty coöperation between the two bodies; and, wherever there is such wise and hearty coöperation, the faculty will have very large influence in the counsels and acts of the government. This influence, however, ought, in those cases where the University at large is concerned, to be the combined influence of all the faculties. But in order to this end, there must be not infrequent meetings of the several faculties as one body. The recommendations made must come from the whole body. The University must be carried forward by a common impulse.

As a *third* means of accomplishing the unifying work, of which we have spoken, we mention the raising of a large fund for *the University*. Efforts made heretofore for the collection of money have always been put forth for some specific object or for some special department. Such efforts have been repeated, from time to time, and have met with gratifying success. They have proved beneficial to the whole institution, in so far as they have strengthened one or another of its larger or smaller parts. But no general and wide-extended plan has been entered upon, which should embrace all the departments and should continue until its complete accomplishment, no matter how long a period might be required for that end. The need of such a plan, and of an energetic prosecution of it, we believe, is apparent. Every other plan, involving efforts only in a single line, must be partial in its character. Two or three such partial plans, if entered upon at the same time, may interfere with one another's success in considerable degree. If, on the other hand, in order to avoid such collision, they are entered upon successively, a large amount of valuable time may be lost for one portion of the University in waiting for another. Yale College, too, can speak to its alumni and its friends with more emphasis and impressiveness than can any of its separate departments by itself. Moreover, the other methods have been tried by themselves long enough, and everything is now propitious for a general movement for the general interests. What has been already done has shown that there is a vast amount of money in the country, held by persons who are desirous of using it for the highest benevolent ends. It has, also, become equally clear, that energy in the work of making known the wants of the College and the good it is accomplishing will be rewarded. The story of the necessities and the work of this institution has never failed to meet a favorable response from the generosity of many benefactors. And, from the experience of years past, we are constrained to bear testimony, that the want of a more perfect supply of the needs of the College is owing as largely to the want of constant and untiring energy in the work of solicitation, as to that of willingness on the part of men, who fully understand the case, to give with liberality. Giving, we are well aware, is a slow work for most men. Asking men to give is a still harder work. But the man whose cause is a good one, and who does not grow faint-hearted in his labors, will, finally, receive full measure for the asking. We know this, because we have been associated intimately with a small circle of men who have been asking for one of the good causes of this institution. They have been earnest in their labors, but they might have been more so, and we have no more doubt of their having attained a far greater success, if they had been, than we have of the success already gained. Yale College is the largest and highest educational institution, under real and pronounced Christian influences, in the country. It has a past history of nearly two hundred years. Its graduates, in the past, have been among the noblest men in the former generations. Its living alumni are scattered everywhere through the land. They are men of eminence, of large means, of Christian usefulness, of wide-spread influence. Its friends are more numerous than either they or itself know. What cause is better than its cause? What asking will meet a readier and heartier answer than its asking? Why should it not ask for all that it needs now?

There have been, as we conceive, two unfortunate things, in respect to this matter, in the history of this institution. The first is a despondent feeling as to the likelihood of success, if solicitations should be made, and the second, which is closely allied to the other, is a shrinking from a constant and earnest pressing of the wants of the College on the attention of those interested in it. We hope that the many gifts, which have been received in recent years, may, gradually at least, remove these things in the future. Certainly the work of the future cannot be accomplished unless they are removed. A grand, combined movement, which shall appeal to and interest every friend of the College and every graduate of any of its departments, is the thing which is needed. The widely extended impression, that the College is wealthy—even with a superabundance of riches,—must be carefully counteracted by repeated presentations of the facts of the case. The specific wants must be made known with all clearness and fullness. Men must be urged to give to anything which awakens their special interest; and all, who will do so, must be urged to give to the general fund of the whole University. When this general fund is gathered in, it must, if the end of which we speak is to be attained, be divided among the several departments according to their need. Everything must be done with a view to the common good of all. This work, also, must be entered upon not for a few months, but for years. The enlistment must be for a long period; and, under the guidance of the central power, every man, who can be called on to aid, must be summoned to do good service in the cause. The sum aimed at must be a large one—sufficient to cover all necessities. The age is ready for large things, and more likely to do them than it is to do small ones. And there must be no faltering or faintheartedness to the very end. There is no real occasion for any such feeling, for the dangers of failure in this matter are such as always pass away before a determined energy. There is not a department of the University, we verily believe, which,—starting, by itself alone, with a heroic energy worthy of its cause,—would not obtain, within a single year, an amount of aid surprising, in its largeness, both to itself and to all its friends. Doubt and the weakness of effort which follow upon it are the worst of enemies in such a cause. They bring their own defeat—a defeat just proportioned to their magnitude.

If such a fund should be raised for the University—and that it can be, in case the work be undertaken in the spirit and with the energy indicated above, all the lessons of our past experience, so far as they teach anything, clearly show—and if, as and after it is raised, it should be divided according to the dictates of those feelings which, as we have said, ought to characterize the new era, it would greatly help the University to grow in all its parts, and to become what it ought to be. There are departments here, which are suffering, to-day, beyond measure because they are almost entirely without funds. They ought to be provided for, first and most carefully, in such a distribution. The attention of the governing powers ought to be at once and earnestly given to them, that they may be strengthened according to their necessities. When this is done, every other section of the University—every minor branch of every department of it—should have its wants thoroughly investigated and proportionately provided for. We believe that a million of dollars can be collected from the friends and graduates of Yale for the promotion of its means of instruction within the next ten years. We believe that measures should be at once introduced, looking toward the accomplishment of this result, and that those whose proper office it is to institute and carry out these measures should say to themselves continually, "There is for us no such word in the English language as *failure.*" We believe that every year's delay in this matter is a loss of opportunity, and an endangering of the final issue. The present is a golden period. It is being taken advantage of on every hand. If men here defer their working, or go forward with little efficiency, other men, elsewhere, will bear away the rewards, because of their greater promptness and vigor. We hope the new era will be one of as much energy in respect to the gathering in of funds to the treasury of Yale, as the past has been of skill in the management of funds already gathered in—that the new era will be one of forth-putting power, and will not exhaust itself on what it already has. But, however great may be the results, if they are not used with a true impartiality towards all the departments—if they are devoted to the collegiate school alone—the University-life will die away or be destroyed, and its destruction will be owing to the want of any true idea of what the University is, or any true desire to have it grow in power. We can hardly persuade ourselves that the friends and governors of Yale College will, in any such way, reject the possibilities, which are offered them, of making this institution one of the great Universities of the country. If they do, they will prove themselves unworthy sons of those noble men, who, in the day of small things at the beginning of this century, had a vision of the possible future, and, with their scanty means, provided for the realization, at a later period, of what they saw only in the distant prospect.

We add, as a *fourth* means of bringing the whole institution into unity, and, thus, of accomplishing the work of the new era, a suggestion as to the chief office of the University. The President of Yale College is the presiding officer of the Board of Trustees, and is the head of the faculty of each and every department. He is, thus, the one person who, according to the theory of the institution, meets with and forms the center of all the official bodies within it. In the practical working of the institution, however, the theory is not fully carried out. The institution, in this point as in all others, feels the influence of its origin. It began as a collegiate school, with its presiding officer as one of its teachers. When, in subsequent times, other schools were added to the original one, new bodies of instructors were appointed for their peculiar work, but the President did not extend his teachings into these new departments. In this respect he has always been limited, (except, indeed, in the giving of a few lectures, in special cases, of late years,) to the college or academical branch of the institution. He has met with the faculty of that branch only, in their regular meetings, and his work has been mainly in association with them. Having so many duties in that department—more, even, at times, than ought to be imposed upon any single man—he has scarcely been able to take upon himself similar duties in other departments. The necessities of the case have made him, in reality, the president of one faculty only, while, in name, he has been the head of all. If we look back thirty or forty years, we doubt whether the College President ever, (except in the most extraordinary emergencies,) sat in session with the officers of the professional schools. In later times, such meetings have been more frequent, but, even now, they take place only at long intervals, while with the academical faculty he has one session in every week. The difference is owing to the impossibility that one man should do everything. Human powers cannot go beyond certain bounds; and, so long as the President has, in the college department, daily recitations to hear and daily lectures to give, and all the work upon his hands of what is known to college men as a "division" officer (involving the hearing of excuses and other such petty duty,) and is, it would seem, almost an office-clerk for everybody to write to or to call upon, it can scarcely be demanded of him that he should give himself largely to the professional and scientific schools. But, if he does not devote himself to all, and meet with all the faculties, the inevitable result will be, that he will not have the same minute knowledge of the life and wants of all,—and the almost inevitable result will be, that his personal interest in all cannot be like that which he has in the one department, into immediate connection with whose daily life he is constantly brought. He must be a larger-minded and larger-hearted man than most men are, if he is able to overcome these limitations which beset him, and to feel, at all times, that every department of the University is just as important as his own. But, if he does not feel this,—inasmuch as he is the center of power and influence, and the sole representative of the faculties in the corporation—the other schools will, sooner or later, suffer in comparison with the one to which he especially belongs; and the danger of this result will be increased, because the officers of that school have nearer and more constant access to him than those of any other.

Yale College has become a wide-extended institution. Its growth, within the last twenty-five years, has been very great. It seems to us a question worthy of the most serious consideration, whether it has not become so large as to require the old system of things to be modified. Is it not time, or is not the time approaching—we do not say *it is*, but *is it not*—when the chief office in the University shall be changed in its character, and shall no longer bear such a special relation to a single department? Does not the work of the new era, which is to change the institution from a College with outside schools into a University composed of coördinate and coequal branches, require for its accomplishment that the head of the institution shall have precisely the same relation to all the branches? We have, already, seen that there is work enough, and more than enough, for such an officer as the academical department needs to preside over its affairs. But to those who thoughtfully observe the common life and interests of the whole University we believe it is equally clear, that there is work enough connected with those common interests to occupy the mind and the time of the ablest man who can be found to perform it. If, however, this be so, it becomes, to say the least, an important point of inquiry whether the first-mentioned work should not be done by a dean of the academical faculty, (with similar officers in the other faculties, so far as needed,) while the President should be connected alike with all faculties *in reality* as well as *in name*, and should have especial charge of the great common interests and life. Of the uniting power of such an office—of its immediate tendency to promote the growth of the University as distinguished from the College—it would seem that there could scarcely be any doubt. Unless, therefore, some weightier argument from some other source can be brought against such a change in the constitution of affairs, it ought to be made. And to the consideration of the whole question the minds of the governing powers, as it seems to us, may well be given at the proper moment. Why should not the next administration begin with the assignment of these new duties to the highest officer of the institution? Certainly, at some time in the new era, this matter will press itself, and, we can hardly doubt, will be decided in favor of the change. All that we would hope is, that its discussion may not be deferred so long as to lose any advantages to the University in consequence.

The change here referred to need not, as it seems to us, and ought not to diminish the intellectual or religious influence of the President upon the students of the University. It might, even, increase that which should be exerted upon those belonging to the other departments beyond the academical. The President, in our view, ought never to be a mere business agent of the University. He should have some share in the instruction of the students, and should have the opportunity of coming in contact with them. Otherwise, the office will have less attraction for men of eminent intellectual ability, and, on the other hand, there will be a great loss of possible good influence. His very office gives the President—if he meets them and they know him in the class-room—two or three times the power with the students, which even the same man would have as one of the professors. This power ought to be used. But it is not essential to his discharging the duties of instruction, that he should be confined to the collegiate department. He can be a University lecturer, lecturing on subjects which are of importance and interest to the students of all the schools. He can give different courses, to a certain extent, adapted more particularly to the wants of each of the separate schools. If he is set apart by ordination to the office of the ministry, as always has been, and we hope always will be, the case in this institution, he can preach frequently in the University Chapel, or meet the students in their special or general meetings of a religious character. We know of no nobler work—more worthy of the highest powers, or more truly honorable for a man who is fitted for it—than to stand thus at the center of a great and growing University, with his heart and mind open to the wants of its every department—with his efforts ready to bear it forward in all parts alike—with the influence of his character and the impress of his intellectual power coming upon every student who finds his way anywhere within its walls. The constantly increasing fame of the institution would be his fame. The lives of thousands of students would bear within themselves, and would transmit to a future generation the lessons which they learned from him. His office would be even a higher and better one than it can be now, just in proportion as it would have a wider sphere of working, and a greater end to accomplish. It would be to its former self almost as the University is to the College.

Before closing our consideration of the means of accomplishing the work of unifying the institution more perfectly, we desire to add one or two suggestions of minor importance. One of these is, that, in addition to the present honors given to students of merit in the different departments, there might be established prizes or rewards which should be open to those of all departments. The degree of Doctor of Philosophy is now offered to students of the schools of science and of the higher philosophy and philology. Might not this degree, or some similar mark of distinction, be made a University honor for *all* who should prove themselves worthy of it? Or, if not this, might not university prizes be proposed for all, to be given as the result of examinations in the several lines of study pursued by different classes of students? Of course, from the nature of the case, such rewards could not be offered to undergraduates in the department of arts or in that of science, because they do not stand upon a common level with the graduated students who are found in the professional schools and the higher and more professional branch of the scientific department. But this exclusion of such undergraduates would be incidental to their position, and it would be no injustice to or real exclusion of the departments to which they belong, because each of these departments extends itself into the higher schools of philology and science already referred to. There would, therefore, be nothing in such a plan to oppose the University idea, but, on the other hand, there would be everything to favor it, and more perfectly carry it out. Such a plan would, of course, require careful thought before its adoption. Difficulties in the way of its successful accomplishment might present themselves, at first. But it is deserving of consideration and, as we are inclined to believe, will demand consideration in the coming years. If it is wise to adopt the plan, the influence of its adoption on the end which we now have in view—namely, the establishment and growth of the University as distinguished from the mere college, or the making of the University to be one body with coördinate branches—is almost beyond question. In this way, the University will appeal to all its students alike, and they will feel that they are united in one company.

Another suggestion which may be offered is, that the graduates of all the departments should be regarded equally as sons of the University. This is the case already, in a certain measure. The students who have completed their course of study in the various schools are recorded in the general catalogue of the college. But it is evident to every observer, that those whom the college regards as its alumni, in the full sense of the word, are the graduates of the academical department only. This sentiment is a growth of all the past history of the institution and of the way, already pointed out, in which it has become what it is. A College, which has, so to speak, taken on, in the progress of years, certain outside schools, will naturally feel itself to be the central and essential thing. It will claim for its graduates the privileges of the household. It will look upon others as only holding an inferior place. Every one of these graduates will look upon himself as belonging to the innermost circle, and will appropriate to himself the name of the institution in a sense in which he concedes it to no other. But, so long as this continues to be the case, the University spirit will suffer in its development. The insensible but inevitable influence of such feelings in the academical department and its graduates upon the other departments will be a depressing influence. Their graduates will see that they are regarded as a less privileged order; and, because they are not of the collegiate school, they will lose something of the spirit of the place. The recent years have, already, witnessed a considerable change in this respect. The growth in numbers, or in what we may call the "institutional" life, of some of the other schools has, in a measure, broken in upon the old feeling, and we anticipate in the future a far more complete change. And why should there not be such a change? The student in theology or law is pursuing a no less noble branch of learning than the student of the pure mathematics or of the ancient languages. The person who enters upon the general course in the scientific department, whatever may be thought of the comparative value of the education he receives, is as truly a son of the University as the one who gives himself to the regular course of the department of arts. The old idea has had a very natural origin and growth, but it is, nevertheless, a false one. Every man graduating at Harvard or Yale—whatever degree he may have taken—is a son of Harvard or Yale. He ought to have all the privileges of such sonship. He ought to be recognized everywhere as on an equality, as a graduate, with every other; and we are sure that he will be hereafter. Of the uniting influence upon the life of the university of his being thus recognized, we say again, as we have, already, repeatedly said in other connections, there can be no doubt.

We suggest further, as another step in the same direction, the adoption of the name *University*. There has been a sort of satisfaction, we confess, in the minds of the friends of this institution, that it has always had the name of *College*. So long as schools of scarcely the dignity of our higher academies, and with no pretence to any department except the collegiate, and with not even students enough for a respectable class, are calling themselves universities, it is pleasant to think that a great institution like Yale has always kept its old unpretending name. But if we look at the facts of the case, the time has passed for the appropriateness of this title. It no longer describes what the institution really is. It creates endless confusion, because the word *College* must be used in two senses,—at one time, referring to the academical department only, and, at another, to all the departments as united together. A man may thus be a professor or a student in the college and not in the college at the same time, and what the college is becomes a matter of uncertainty to the outside world. It tends, also, to give the collegiate branch the preëminence above all others and to perpetuate the want of coördination among the various schools. Names are very important, oftentimes. They represent things. They are, as it were, the things themselves. They ought, therefore, to be given according to the nature of the things. Yale College, as a mere college, is only a part—it is only one of five branches of the institution which is known by that name. There is a university at New Haven, which includes the college, which has grown out of, indeed, but far beyond the limits of the college. Why should it not designate itself by a name which is suited to distinguish its peculiar character? It is a university—why should it not be called one? But, whatever may be the desirableness or undesirableness of adopting this name on other grounds, it appears to us that its adoption must tend to the accomplishment of the object of uniting the departments by a common bond. These various departments would, at once, become, to their own apprehension and the apprehension of the world, members of the one body—members with equal privileges and an equal rank. The constant use of the new title would be a continual reminder to all of their relations to one another, and would be a sort of outward manifestation and declaration of the true idea of the university.

These last mentioned suggestions, as we have intimated, may be considered of minor importance, as compared with those which were previously presented. They are not, however, without weight. The institution is not beginning now, without any old traditions. It is bearing in its life the influences of a history of nearly two hundred years. These influences, so far as the point now before us is concerned, have been largely in a direction opposite to the university idea. They must, therefore, be counteracted, if that idea is to gain its proper place. Everything may well be done, under such circumstances, which, by any means, can remove the wrong notions and establish the right one. Even names, and things of inferior consequence, if they will prove helpful to the end, may wisely be cared for, and, as it appears to us, those who may have in charge the great and special work of the coming era should thoughtfully consider every measure which may bear upon this work; and if, after such consideration, any means, even the least, shall seem adapted to bring the end in view, they should promptly decide to use them.

The American University—in the highest sense of that word—is a thing of the future. But it is not to be originated in the future. It is not to be established by the resolutions of a mass convention, or by the efforts of a few reformers in education, whose only aim is to overthrow established systems, and all whose ideas are the outgrowth of modern American society. It will have its life rooted in the past. It will have a historic character. Where it will be located, or whether there will be one institution, or more than one, which will deserve and bear the name, it may be presumptuous, at this period of the country's progress, to attempt to determine. But it is not too much to say, that those great institutions which have been growing in strength and solidity and numbers for two centuries have many advantages over all others in respect to the coming time. They have a past history, which is secure. They have the traditions of the past to hold them to a true conservatism. As they are not the creatures of the present, they need not succumb to the passing notions of the hour.

They can pass, in their life, from all the sound thoughts of former generations to the still higher ideals of scholarship of a coming age—and can take from the present, as they pass onward, only that measure of its influence which is good. Their growth is the only healthy growth—that which starts from the beginning of the nation's life and keeps steadily on into the indefinite future. So far as the possibilities of human vision go, therefore, we may predict for them—if their course is directed by wisdom—more safely than for any others, the realization of this high idea. Surely, every friend of theirs and every well-wisher of his country ought to desire for them this honorable future, for it will be a glory to the nation if its noblest and highest universities are, in all time, those which have grown with its growth and strengthened with its strength. But, if they are to attain this end, they cannot linger in the sphere of *mere colleges.* They cannot neglect the development of any of their parts, but must see that all the parts increase together in the unity and harmony of a common life. A grave responsibility will rest upon those who have the positions of authority in them in the coming years. It will be, however, as in all great works, a responsibility only commensurate with the good to be accomplished and the reward to be attained. We believe that the time is close at hand when the University idea must be taken as the true guiding thought of all the future—when the old notion of a college with minor schools attached to it must be abandoned forever, and the several departments must be regarded as altogether coequal—when all portions of the institution must be pressed forward with the same energy, and watched over with the same minute and constant care—or the hope of the future will fail. Other institutions of later origin and less noble past history will take the honor which is ready and waiting now for these.

We have spoken of Yale College because we are deeply interested in it. Much of what we have said would apply elsewhere, but our thoughts and those of our associates are naturally upon the future of our own University. We hope that that future may be marked by wisdom as great as has characterized the past. Through the wisdom of the past, the institution has grown from its small beginnings, in the times of the early fathers, to the greatness of its present numbers and the wideness of its present fame. It has developed itself outward from its original center into new departments as they were needed, until now it is a complete University *in its plan and form.* It needs only that continual growth, which is the necessity of all life, and that more perfect unity of all its parts which shall impart to it still greater strength and vigor for its future course, in order to make it all that its most ardent friends could desire it to become—*a complete University in the highest sense.*

SECOND ARTICLE.

In the preceding Article, we have considered the work of the new era, on which the College is about to enter, so far as relates to the unifying of the institution, or the making it to be no longer a Collegiate school, with certain "outside" departments loosely attached to the central body, but a University of coördinate and coequal branches. This work of unification is the first work that should be undertaken and carried out. It is essential to the noblest growth of the institution, and it is essential that it be done at once. It is, therefore, most proper that, in any discussion respecting the coming era, this subject should hold the first and most prominent place. But it is only one among a number of important things which need to be accomplished. We trust it will not be deemed out of place, therefore, if we ask the attention of our readers, at the present time, to another point connected with this most interesting subject—the work to be done in the future.

The suggestion which we would now make is with reference to suitable provisions and arrangements for those "graduated" students who are pursuing a general and non-professional course of study. This class of persons have peculiar claims on the care and interest of the governing powers of the institution, whatever may be the light in which we look at them. To those who think only of the collegiate or academical department, and believe the other schools to be of little or no importance, the young men, who, having just taken their first degree in arts, propose to continue their past studies, can hardly fail to be objects of regard. The existence of such a body of young men residing at the college is an honor to their instructors, as well as a continual inspiration to the undergraduates who are following them. To those, on the other hand, who have larger views and who wish for a university, such graduates are of still greater consequence. They form one of *the essential parts* of the university, without which its life cannot, by any means, be complete. And even to those—if any such there can be—who have no care for the character and form of our higher institutions of learning, but yet desire the progress of literature and scholarly refinement in the country, it will be a matter of no slight moment to give this class of students the greatest advantages, since on them must largely depend all hopes which go out towards this end. And yet it is not strange that they have been the latest class, even of graduate students, to be provided for. Our country has made but slow progress, in the past, towards the higher regions of literary refinement. Another and more fundamental work has been essential to its earlier life. The various learned professions have, indeed, long since become necessary, and, accordingly, provision has been made at our educational institutions for those who would enter them. But scholarship, in those other fields which are less immediately connected with the every-day work of life, has been left to the older nations. Its importance has not been appreciated as if it were a thing of present need. There has, consequently, been little demand for it in the public mind, and little or no facilities for attaining it have been offered, even in those colleges which have begun to develop themselves outward toward the university idea. Within the last few years, however, there has been a great advance in this direction. We have begun to feel that our country must not be a place for the exercise of practical energy, merely, and that learning must not be limited to those alone who are lawyers or preachers, but that we must be a nation of the truest and noblest culture—that scholars must find their home here, and must be honored here, as truly as in Europe. The call for a higher education in this field has, therefore, begun to arise. Our universities must have a department not only separate from the collegiate school, but also from the professional schools, which shall draw into itself many of the best minds and carry them onward in their scholarly culture. It is one of the honors of Yale College, that its governors were among the earliest, if not the very earliest, in the country to hear this call. When it had come only from two or three, as it were, scattered here and there—when the great body even of our educated countrymen had no sense, as yet, of the need of any such thing—they organized a new branch of the institution for these higher liberal studies. The Department of Philosophy and the Arts was created in 1846. It opened the way for the pursuit of natural science in its various departments, thus meeting the demands of the times in this direction. But, at the same time, it offered more advanced instruction in philosophy, and philology, and history, and similar studies to the graduates in arts, and to others who might desire it.

Of what this Department, in what we may call its philosophical and philological branch, has already accomplished, very favorable testimony has been borne by the presiding officer of our sister university at Cambridge. Persons among our own graduates, who, in years past, have enjoyed the advantages it affords,—as one of the number, the writer of these Articles—can bear, from their own experience, a witness which, if not as honorable, is, if possible, even more heartfelt. But how little, we must all say, has it done, as yet, compared with what could be desired. How great is the work which opens before it in the future. In organizing this Department of Philosophy and the Arts, the College authorities, as we intimated in our former Article, made the institution *complete in its parts.* They gave to the growing University the Philosophical Faculty of the German Universities. But they were unable to do anything more than this—except in the Scientific section of it, where the wonderful developments and demands of the age have carried forward the growth very rapidly. The want of the necessary funds rendered it impossible to make this faculty altogether distinct from the academical, and the want of appreciation of high scholarship in these philosophical and philological studies made the number of students a very limited one. A quarter of a century has, therefore, passed away, and we still see only the small beginnings—two or three young men entering this section of the Department from year to year, and no instruction except from professors who are overburdened with other work. All honor to the Trustees of the College, it becomes all its friends and all the friends of education to say, that they saw so early, and made so early provision for, the new needs of the country. All honor, also, to the instructors for what they have accomplished under circumstances no more favorable than have been, as yet, enjoyed. But no one can fail to see that the work of this part of the institution is, mainly, a work of the coming era. Much more must be done, in the future years, than has hitherto been done, or the guardians of the interests of the University hereafter will, in this regard, prove unequal in wisdom and energy to those who preceded them.

But the great question, as we enter on the new era, is, *what* is to be its work. What then, *in this department* of which we are now speaking, is to be done, to promote its efficiency and to make it in reality what it already is in name? The first thing, as we conceive, is to provide further instruction. All that is now done is to offer assistance in their studies in the higher Philosophy, Mathematics and Philology, to such young men of proper previous attainments as may desire it. This assistance is to be given by Professors who have duties, which afford them abundant employment, in the academical or scientific schools. In the practical working of the matter, therefore, the necessary tendency of things is to make it as small as possible. *To a large extent*, at the present time, it does not amount to positive instruction, but is only a permission given to the student to call on and consult the professor, when occasion may require. Such a permission is a far smaller advantage than it might seem to be at first sight, for it must be remembered that the professors are known to be pressed with other work, and the students, having most of them just graduated from the college, and having, thus, hardly escaped their feeling of awe towards the older members of the faculty, will scarcely approach the instructors with the perfect freedom that could be wished. The Professor gives his invitation, indeed, but the student either knows, or feels, that it is given with a certain reservation. An overworked man, he says to himself, who sets me no particular time for visiting him—whom I may find, when I call at his room, occupied with other things, or even with other students—the necessity of whose life compels him, it may be, to do much outside of his own special sphere, in order to support his family—such a man cannot wish to see me often. He makes his offer of advice and help with as good heart as may be possible, under the circumstances. I do not doubt this—but he cannot but be glad to have the time, which I should take from him, unbroken. I will wait for another day. I will pass over the present need. I will get on by myself as best I can. It is almost inevitable that he will reason thus, not once, but many times. These thoughts will rise as a hindrance in his way almost as often as he feels the want of assistance, and the result will be that his visits to his instructor will become very infrequent—perhaps, even more and more infrequent, the longer his course of study continues. The offered aid will be unused, and the student will be left to himself. Now we do not say, at this point of our discussion, that anything better could have been done in the past. We have been in the early days—the beginnings—and it is enough that the beginnings have been made. We must not look for the full completion of the plan, as yet. But—with every allowance and with no disposition to find fault—it must be admitted that this condition of things cannot last, if the institution is to grow, and to become what it may be and ought to be. There must be not only the offer of advice and assistance, when it is sought for; there must be definite and regular instruction, with responsibility on the part of the student. There must be lectures or recitations in connection with these studies as regularly as in the theological and law schools. There must be somewhat of systematic organization, or there will be no permanent and large success.

A much more regularly organized section of the university is the first thing which, as it seems to us, is required, if proper provision is to be made for the class of graduated students, to which we are referring. We shall not, of course, be misunderstood as urging any prescribed course of study for all the students, or any abridgment of personal freedom. This we have no wish for, and, certainly, it cannot be regarded as essential. But the section, whether it has ten students or fifty, should have an organized life, and its instruction should be systematic and positive,—as much so as in the case of any other of the higher departments of the University.

In order to the accomplishment of this end, it is of the highest importance that new professorships should be established, the incumbents of which should have no duties outside of this particular section. If the time of a Professor of Greek is needed for the instruction of students in the undergraduate department, who are in the rudiments and the early stages,—

surely, the graduates, who wish to enter more fully into the genius of the language, and to become real scholars, ought not to be compelled to help themselves altogether, except so far as they may snatch an hour or two from his scanty leisure. They ought to have the highest order of instructor whom the University can command—a man who should be devoted to them, as fully as they may need him. The leading Greek scholar in the whole institution should be with them. And so, in the case of the other branches of study. If we are ever to hope for the highest scholarship in this country—if we are ever to give to culture its own proper place—we must accomplish the end in this way. We must not linger in the lower regions and give our thoughts wholly to the younger students. We must make the more full and complete provision for those who are pressing further onward and are to do most in their work.

But it will, doubtless, be said, that, while all this is very good as a theory, it cannot be accomplished for lack of funds. Professorships cannot be established without money, and there is no money. We, however, are speaking of the future—of the work of the opening era—and, as we have already stated, one of the great things to be done in that era is to get money for the whole University. If the officers and friends of this college are to sit down in despair, with the feeling that its pecuniary resources cannot be enlarged, they might as well abandon their work at once. This is the essential thing for future progress, and it can be obtained, if judiciously and earnestly sought. Our suggestions are made on the assumption that this vital necessity is to be secured; and we say, that, on this assumption, these new professorships are imperatively required. The instruction in the higher philology and philosophy, cannot be left, always, to professors of the academical or other departments, who are assigned to this *extra* duty, in addition to the performance of all their other work. As well might the theological school hope to reach its highest growth with no professors of its own. The remnants of a man's time and strength, after his daily labor is ended, are not and never can be sufficient for the greatest work possible to his powers. And yet, we must, of course, freely admit that a time must intervene before these new professorships can be established. It may be, at the best, some years before the funds of the University can be thus largely augmented. A present necessity must, therefore, be looked at, and we must inquire how the efficiency of this section of the institution can, even now, be increased. The course already adopted at Harvard University, gives a hint, at least, as to what may be done. So far as we understand the Harvard scheme, it seems to us to be open to some objections, but its introduction is an evidence of the energy and wisdom of the President of that institution. Lectures of a somewhat similar character, though more exclusively designed for Uinversity students, might be given by the leading professors at Yale; and more familiar exercises might be added, in which the students should come into personal connection with these professors, and should discuss with them the topics of interest connected with their studies or reading. Other eminently-qualified persons might, also, to a certain extent, be called in from outside of the college, to aid in the work. The range of subjects might be a wide one, and such as would interest and stimulate a large number of minds. The fees for attendance on these lectures might be fixed at such a sum as would not be burdensome to the hearers, and, thus, would not shut out those of limited means. In this way, some slight compensation could be made to the instructors—but we can hardly doubt that the satisfaction of seeing the enthusiasm of the students, and the growth of their numbers, would be a sufficient reward, until the time of more abundant resources should come. The gentlemen—at least, those among them who were connected with the University, and we should say that these ought to be the larger or the more efficient part—might meet together as a faculty, and, in this way help and encourage one another. We are persuaded that—while entire success cannot be attained, until new professorships, as indicated above, are established—a great deal more can be done, than has yet been done, with the means already at our disposal. In a few years, with such arrangements and others which can be devised, we cannot doubt, that the number of young men who would enter upon these courses of study, instead of being two or three as now, would be ten or twenty times as many. They would be not only graduates of this college, but graduates of other colleges as well, who would gladly come here to carry onward their education in the midst of these higher advantages. They would be representatives of every class in the country, who wish to gain a culture which they have never yet gained and cannot gain elsewhere. Why should not this step be taken at once? The present is as favorable a time as can ever offer, for the first onward movement. If it is made, not only will great good be done to many individual minds, and to the University as a whole; but the manifestation of energy and the beginning of success will render the gathering in of funds for the future and for the more perfect work a thing both easier and more certain of accomplishment. Men love to see success, and to make it still more successful. To him that hath shall be given, is a principle of the widest application.

There are, however, some other things which may be done, besides the providing of further instruction. Encouragements and helps may be given to students, and, thus, the number of students may be increased. According to the present arrangement of things, no certain advantages are offered to young men entering upon this course of study. The present aids of a pecuniary nature are less, even, than those afforded to undergraduates, while the prospects for the future are, by no means, so sure as those opened before the professional and scientific students. We think something may be done, and ought to be done, within a few years, with reference to both of these points. At present, all which the college has, to give, in this section of the department of Philosophy and the Arts, is the income of three scholarships—the largest income of the three being only one hundred and twenty dollars. After the payment of the annual fee for instruction, the student who holds this best of the scholarships finds himself with only twenty dollars as the proceeds of it. Certainly, an aspiring and enthusiastic youth—whose means are limited—will not find much encouragement to continue his classical or philosophical studies from such a source as this. He will feel himself compelled to give up these studies of his choice, and enter upon some other course, which may either afford him greater assistance at once, or, at least, may compensate him by the larger rewards which it will secure to him in after years. The present inducements of this character we may, therefore, say are nothing. So far as our knowledge extends, no one has ever been led to remain at Yale College, after graduation, by these existing scholarships. But little competition has been known in the case of that one among them, the income of which has depended altogether upon continued residence at New Haven. It has been sought for only by those who, on other grounds, had determined upon this course, and has by them been regarded as a matter of not much moment. Twenty dollars or a hundred and twenty, in these days, are not worth much striving for—and the honor of obtaining that for which there is no competition, is not great enough to call forth any considerable effort or enthusiasm. The founders of these scholarships deserve the credit of their work, and, especially, of their appreciation of this great need of the University. But the coming era cannot be content with no greater things than these. The establishment of fellowships, which shall produce, according to the common phrase, "a living income," is a matter of the highest importance. The foundation of each of these fellowships should be from ten to fifteen or twenty thousand dollars. The time of holding them, also, should be lengthened from two years, as in the case of the existing scholarships, to four—or even six years. They would, thus, become really valuable, and would be a powerful stimulus to many minds. Even one such fellowship, opening itself to competition in every year, would be of the greatest possible service. It would benefit not only the successful candidate, but others likewise. It would, in many cases, be the means of drawing both the unsuccessful and the successful ones into this section of the University. The means for such foundations should be earnestly solicited. They can be secured, as we believe, at no very distant day.

But here again we must admit that there will be an interval of time before this result can be reached. Cannot anything be done in this interval? Perhaps not in the way of pecuniary aid. In other ways, however, we are sure that a beginning may be made at once. It appears to us, that the prospects for the future for this class of students might be rendered much brighter and more certain than they now are. At present, a young man in this department of study is in the most uncertain of all positions. He has not a fraction of the ground for confidence respecting an opening for the exercise of his powers in after life, which a lawyer or a minister may have. This, no doubt, is largely owing to circumstances beyond control. The age of scholarly culture is only just dawning, and the places for scholarly men are comparatively few. We do not see, however, why the Tutorships or Assistant Professorships in the college might not be regularly filled from students of this class. On the present system, the elections to the Tutorship are made from among the highest on the list of "appointments" at Commencement. Two or three years after graduation, the valedictorian or salutatorian of a class is called to this office of instruction, because he had such a rank as a scholar in his college course, and because the Faculty judge, from what they remember of him, that he will discharge its duties well. It can be no wonder, surely, if, on such a system, mistaken choices are sometimes made. Valedictorians are, now and then at least, not distinguished as real scholars, when they graduate. They are, by no means, certain to be so three years afterwards—and even less certain to be good teachers. But if this important office of instruction is filled in the way we suggest, the candidates will be all of them persons who are known to be continuing their studies, and to be making real progress. They can be observed by the college authorities, as they go forward. The best among them can be chosen. The appointment can become a reward, the hope of which will make all of them as good as possible. An arrangement of this character will tend toward beneficial results for the college itself, while it will, at the same time, encourage the students of the Department. It will encourage them, because these students, looking as they naturally will towards an academic or literary life, will hold such an official position in very different esteem from their college classmates who become doctors or merchants. They will find here a stepping-stone to a higher position, or a preparation for their chosen course of life. The authorities of the College might, also, systematically aid, as far as in their power,—and might let it be distinctly known that they would aid,—these students to obtain places as teachers, or other more purely literary posts, elsewhere. It cannot be doubted, that this is the class of men who ought to be teachers. The growth and needs of the country are such, now, that teaching is beginning to be as much a profession as the ministry is. Why should not the profession be filled, like that of the ministry, from those who have been specially educated for it?

If, in these ways, the prospects for the future of these graduate students could be made more certain than they now are, the influence of such greater certainty would be, undoubtedly, to increase the number of young men who would thus devote themselves to general studies. Our Universities must, it is true, wait for their highest success and most perfect development, until the demands of the country are greater. But they must educate the country, continually, towards the higher demands, by keeping steadily in advance of the present public sentiment. They must provide every inducement, which they can, even now, and must furnish all possible aid, if they are to fulfill their mission. It is thus, that they are to prepare the way for the better future, as well as to be ready for it when it comes.

There is another thing, which, we think, can be done, and done immediately, for the growth and success of this section of the University. Students, if they are to enter upon these higher studies in philosophy and philology, need not only the encouragements of present aid and future rewards. They need, also, *an inspiration* to make them ready to choose the course, which thus offers itself to them. They need, *in their undergraduate life*, to have *their love for the studies awakened*, so that they shall be glad to go forward in them. Especially is this the case in the classical languages. Young men, at the age of graduation, are somewhat prone to like mental and moral philosophy—studies which make them realize, more than any others, the intellectual powers just maturing within them—while, in regard to the mathematics, the gift for these is a comparatively rare one, and is usually accompanied, where it exists, by its own inspiration. The almost universal complaint, on the other hand, is, that there is little enthusiasm for classical studies; and great numbers, even of college graduates, are declaring, largely on this account, we believe, that they ought not to be required in a collegiate course. We do not propose here to discuss the general question respecting these studies. So far as our present purpose is concerned, this question may be settled in either way. It is enough for us to take the general admission, that it is well to have a class of classical students, and, if so, to make them as ardent in their work as possible. But, if this be admitted, everything ought to be done in the Academical department of the University to awaken this ardor in such minds. If there are to be a goodly number of these students in the section devoted to the higher general studies, it must be thus awakened. But how shall this object be accomplished?

A step has been taken at Yale College, already, in connection with this matter, which is likely to be helpful to the end in view. The students are not compelled to go forward, as they were formerly, all together—and, thus, no faster or farther than the slower ones can advance. They are arranged in divisions, according to their scholarship, and the higher ranks make correspondingly greater progress. The results of this experiment—which met objections from some persons of great wisdom, at its first suggestion—have been even more favorable, if we mistake not, than most of the college officers anticipated. But there are other steps which, we think, still need to be taken. The classical languages, as we conceive, are taught with too exclusive reference to what is called "discipline." Now everybody, who knows anything on this subject, knows that these languages, like all others, must be studied and understood in their construction and all their grammatical minutiæ, if they are to be thoroughly acquired. All persons, also, agree, that one of the great advantages of the study of these languages, is the mental discipline which is gained from this sort of investigation of them. But a man will never love a language of which he knows nothing but the grammar. It is doubtful if even the celebrated German professor, who lamented that he had not devoted his life exclusively to the dative case, would have appreciated the beauty of such a study, unless he had learned something beyond this. And it is, by no means, strange, if young men in our colleges, whose minds have been so largely confined to grammatical points,—to analysis of words and similar matters—should, at their graduation, have little enthusiasm for the classical authors, or should, at that time, lay them aside, once for all. How much would men study or enjoy the modern languages of Europe, or even our own, if this were the aim of all their reading? In every other case, we study the grammar for the language, while, in this case, we reverse the process and make the language the means and the grammar the end. We cannot help believing that there is a great mistake here, in the arrangements of our college instruction. The best scholars, even, while they are drilled in analysis and forms and rules, are most tryingly deficient in knowledge of the vocabulary of Latin and Greek. They have not learned to dispense, in any considerable measure, with the dictionary, though they may have the grammatical principles most perfectly at command. Only one-half of the work has been accomplished for them; and, so far as the matter of their enthusiasm is concerned, only that half which is least likely to awaken it. A person who cannot lay aside his German lexicon, but must refer to it a score of times for every page he reads, will, almost certainly, like English better. The scholar in Greek or Latin is subject to the same rule. We fully admit, that, in the case of Greek particularly, we cannot easily hope for such entire freedom from bondage, in this regard, as we often attain in German or in French. Nevertheless, we believe it to be possible that our students should know far more of the vocabulary of the classical languages, at the close of their college course, than they now do; and, just in proportion as they do know more, in this way, will their interest in these languages be increased. And while no one believes in the necessity of grammatical study more than we do, we are ready to go so far as to say, that it is better, in every point of view, for a man to be able to read fluently, at graduation, a dialogue of Plato or a chapter of Tacitus, than it is for him ever to have gained the most accurate knowledge of the exceptions to the rules of Latin prosody. Let us carry forward the grammatical studies as far as we can consistently with other ends—let us demand of the preparatory schools a more perfect drill in this department. But do not let us lose everything else in the pursuit of this one object.

The reading, then, of Greek and Latin, with a view to familiarity with the language as distinguished from the grammar, we believe to be a thing of very essential importance. Our college curriculum ought to include such studying of these languages as should deliver the young men, in some degree, from the bondage of school-boys, and should introduce them to somewhat, at least, of the freedom of real scholars. But not only should this be accomplished. In connection with it, another result should be aimed at, which, under the existing system, is very difficult to be attained. The mind of the student should be awakened to an appreciation of the richness of thought, of the grace, of the rhetorical power, of all that is beautiful in the style of the works which he reads. These things vanish from the sight of him who is searching only amid dry details. They hide themselves in a higher sphere. If we could suppose a person to study the poems of Milton or the writings of Burke, as our young men, in the colleges, too generally study the works of the ancient authors—that is, if he were to read but a page or two a day, with a laborious use of the dictionary, and with his attention almost exclusively turned to the derivation of words, or the construction of sentences, or the force of the smallest particles, how little could we expect him to know of that which gives these celebrated writers their fame! He must read long passages at once—whole poems or orations, it may be—in order that he may understand the authors' plan and thought, and may feel the force of what they say. He must read again and again, and try to possess himself of everything which, under the inspiration and direction of their genius, contributes to the accomplishment of their design. He must study their works as if he were to make them the models for his own imitation. He must enter into their spirit. To know the name of every rhetorical figure, and the history of every word as a mere word, in Shakespeare's Plays, is not to know those Plays as one ought to know them. Certainly, to know them thus is not likely to awaken love for them. And this, not because grammar with all that belongs to it, or with it, is not useful or essential to the highest scholarship, but because there is something higher and freer and more inspiring than grammar. Homer might as easily, as it seems to us, have produced his wonderful poems by thinking only of the force of his own particles, as the student of Homer learn to know or love the beauty of those poems by thinking only of the same thing. It is the letter, here as elsewhere, that kills, and the spirit, alone, that gives true life. We press this point, with something of reiteration even, because we regard it as of so great importance. If our college graduates are to have enthusiasm for classical study—if they are to receive, in their earlier course, the impulse to go onward in these studies after their graduation—if the section of our University, of which we are now speaking, is to be filled with its due proportion of ardent lovers of these ancient languages—this higher (or, if that word be objected to, this more love-inspiring) part of the study must be much more largely cultivated in the undergraduate years. Young men do not love the classics, because they do not appreciate that which is rich and beautiful in them. They do not appreciate this, because they are not, carefully and earnestly, taught concerning it. They are not thus taught, because the established system of teaching has been founded so largely on an opposite theory. In the case of English writers, they know the language so familiarly that they naturally study them with reference to style and thought, and, thus, they come to believe in, and to be enthusiastic for, English studies, while they depreciate Latin and Greek, and think them useless or a wearisome burden. The reason of the opposite feelings, and the means of bringing them to a greater similarity, are not difficult of discovery. There is great force, as we have often thought, in the remark once made by a foreign acquaintance of ours on the comparative merits of Schiller and Shakespeare. He regarded the former, he said, as a greater poet than the latter, and, then, with great simplicity and candor, added, "And the reason is, because I understand Schiller and do not understand Shakespeare." Let us make our college students understand the beauties of the Iliad or the Antigone, as they understand those of the noblest English poems, and they will not be content to give up their classical reading. But they cannot thus understand them, if they study only grammatical rules.

We add still another thing, which we think may be done in the undergraduate course to create and increase enthusiasm for these studies, and, thus, may be to the advantage of that section of the University, of which, in this Article, we are speaking. According to the present system, as it seems to us, the student is confined too entirely to the work of mere recitation. He translates a passage of a few lines; or answers certain questions of his instructor, and this is all. He has little or no opportunity to ask questions himself, or to suggest points of discussion which may have interested his own mind. Only one half, therefore, of what is desirable is accomplished for him. We believe, that the other half is greatly needed. A young man in college, who knows that, in the recitation or lecture-room, he must be limited to those matters which, in carrying forward his own plan, the professor is dwelling upon, will learn to prepare himself for the demands made upon him, but he will not be likely to go beyond the routine of these things. He will follow his teacher and depend wholly upon him, without the independent awakening of his own mind. He will lose the inward stimulus which comes from the knowledge, that every inquiry of his own suggestion can present itself for discussion and decision. But, on the other hand, if the instructor is ready to answer as well as to ask questions, and if time is given for the student to say what his own investigation impels him to say, it is almost beyond a doubt that he will look at points which are outside of any mere routine. He will investigate the difficulties which he meets. He will inquire into this and that topic, which, though not in the immediate line of the daily task set before him, are naturally suggested by it. He will be continually incited to raise questions before his own mind, and to try to answer them, because he knows that, if he cannot answer them after such trial, he will be aided by his instructor. He will be glad to learn new things connected with his study, continually, and, as he is learning them, his love for the study will constantly increase. We cannot help believing, that, under such a system as this, five minds would be awakened to enthusiasm, where one is, at present. And this is what we want. The ends of education are not attained, when a certain kind of mental discipline is given and everything besides this is neglected. The implantation in the soul of love for the study is, perhaps, better than all things else; such a love as will inspire the student to continue his work, in after years, and will make knowledge seem to be a thing infinitely to be desired—a reward compensating for every labor and bringing a most perfect satisfaction. Would that such love might be implanted in the soul of every student! It would be worth the loss, even,—if that were necessary,—of some mental discipline. But it can be gained, as we believe, without any such loss.

It may be said, indeed, that the time is wanting for the accomplishment of both these objects, and that it is better to secure one of them perfectly, than to make but half-way work with both. We admit that the time is very fully occupied. It is for this reason that we think a large increase in the number of instructors, in the academical department, is imperatively required. The students need to be divided into smaller sub-divisions, where there can be freer opportunity for all of which we have spoken. But a beginning can be made, we think, even now. If even one exercise in each week could be taken from the ordinary recitation work and devoted to such discussion or questioning, or if one-fourth part of every recitation hour could be thus employed, the results would more than justify the outlay. At almost any sacrifice the results ought to be secured.

We are not here discussing this point, or the others of which mention has been made in connection with the undergraduate department, with reference to themselves and to their own importance. We have only in view, at the present time, the relation of them to the growth of the higher department of philology and philosophy. It is sufficient, therefore, to hint at what is needed, and to show what would be its bearing on the end to be desired. Another time and place would be more suitable for a full development of the whole subject. We would, only, add that we would not speak exclusively of the classical studies. The same thing may be urged, to a greater or less extent, with regard to every branch which is to be pursued in this higher department. More inspiration and enthusiasm need to be imparted in the earlier course, if there is to be any fullness of growth in the later course. The preparation of this character must be made in the part of the University where the education begins, in order that the part where it is carried onward towards the highest culture, may be enabled to do its work for the greatest number and with the most perfect success. We wish it to be borne in mind, also, that we would not demand too much at once. The changes, which are needed,—if our views are correct,—cannot be made in a moment. The full and satisfactory accomplishment of them will require the progress of years and a large increase of means. A University cannot grow into perfection in a year or in a score of years. It cannot do with ten thousand the work which requires twenty thousand. It must move gradually, and must wait, often, for opportunities and possibilities as yet unrealized. No greater unreasonableness can be manifested than in the way of indiscriminate fault-finding. The men of past generations could not do what we can, and we cannot do, to day, what may be an easy work for those who shall come after us. In our discussion, at this time, we are only endeavoring to show where work is needed and what early steps may be taken now. The coming era has its peculiar work. Its dawning is upon us. How are we to meet it? What courses of action shall we enter upon, and what shall we try to do in each one of them as we first enter upon it?

If we may divide the Department of Philosophy and the Arts into two sections, and, for the purposes of our present thought, call the section devoted to general studies, (not within the field of Natural Science,) the Department of Philosophy—the great work of the coming years, of which we now speak, is the work of strengthening this department. It has had a name to live, thus far. It needs to live in reality. Even in its imperfect state, it has accomplished some praiseworthy results. It needs, with a more perfect organization, to do a larger and better work. *The university needs to grow into completeness, in this section of its life.* And, if it does, it will accomplish for American scholarship—for the refinement and cultivation of the people—in the future, more, perhaps, than any mind can measure or estimate.

We are aware that against all which we have said some persons may urge, that the attempt is useless—that such high education is best obtained in Europe, and that students will, certainly, go there, if they desire it. We believe this to be true, to a certain extent, and we believe that our young men ought to go to those older countries, for this object. But this need not prevent our doing all we can at home. If the Universities abroad are to be better than ours, for a hundred or five hundred years to come, or for all time even, there is still no reason why our own should not be made as good as possible, in every part. The more a young man knows when he goes to the European universities, the more good his sojourn there will accomplish for him. The longer he can study at home—within certain limits—the better it will be for his final success. All of us, who have been in Germany, know how many American students there lose one half, or more than one half, of what they go thither to gain, because of their imperfect preparation for their work. They have not made progress enough at home to know what they need, and, much less, how to get it when they enter upon their course there. There is, as it seems to us, therefore, abundant work for this department of our own University. It will, at least, qualify its students to go abroad, if it cannot secure them what can be given abroad. It will do much to accomplish the result which we think must be hoped for in the future—namely, to keep young men from entering upon the active work of life, before they have escaped their immaturity. The restless spirit which makes us impatient to be preachers or lawyers—to be "settled," as we say, in some great business—as soon as possible after manhood commences, must, it would seem, give way as our nation grows older and more populous. When it does, men will be content to prepare themselves more thoroughly for their work. They will have a broader and larger education than they are now willing to wait for. The wide-spread want of confidence in every man who knows anything in any department, which we see in our country now, will give way to a juster estimate of things. Even public office, it is to be hoped, will open itself only to those who are, in some measure, qualified for it. But all this is not to be secured without any efforts or means for securing it. The popular mind must be educated through the higher education that is given to the more favored classes at the Univerities. The better influences must come from these higher sources. There is, then, as it seems to us, abundant ground for every effort to develop the department of which we speak. It is a way in which we are to move onward towards the completeness of the University itself. It is a way in which we are to gain for culture its true place in the national life. It is a way in which we are to give to many an ardent youth one of the greatest blessings that can be bestowed upon him. It is a way in which—if that result is ever to be attained—we are to put ourselves, at some future time, in this regard, on a level with the European world.

We have referred, in these pages, to this section of our University and to what should be done for it, not because we regard it as of more importance than the professional and scientific schools, or than the Academical department, but because it is the section which, as yet, is least perfectly developed. Elsewhere, we have not only the form, but, in some measure, the actual and successful organization of the parts of the complete University. Here we have the form, but, as yet, little more. The entire working power has been from outside of the section itself, and the results have been very limited. Believing, as we do, that the work of the coming era is that of making the institution no longer a college with outside schools, but a university composed of coördinate and co-equal branches —it becomes us, in any more particular discussion of that work, to consider, at the outset, that branch which has attained the least completeness. If we are deficient, anywhere, in the *form* of the University, certainly, one of the earliest works to which we are called is, to fill out the deficiency. If we have, in any part, the *form* without *the fullness of the reality*, we should, as soon as possible, attempt to reach that fullness. So the great end is to be accomplished. The weaker parts, also, —as we have said in our previous Article,—need the first thought and the most tender care. Do not let us neglect anything, whether it be weaker or stronger—but, while we give thought enough to that which is already moving on successfully, let us bestow especial attention on that which needs helping that it may move at all. This is the part of the wise general, or the wise statesman, or the wise guardian of any work, for the accomplishment of which the varied parts must move on together in a successful way. The officers of a university must obey the great general laws of human life, if they would honorably and usefully discharge their trust. Moreover, this section is the one which, in a certain sense, seems to gather into itself, more than any other, the university spirit. Culture for its own sake, and not merely for its practical *uses*, —culture as a good in itself—this is one of the mottoes of a University. Not to despise, rather to glory in, the *uses* of knowledge and its beneficial influence on mankind—but, at the same time, not to despise, but to glory in, *knowledge as the enrichment of the man's own soul*,—this is the spirit of the halls consecrated to learning. The section of the University, where the student is learning only for learning's sake—where his studies are, least of all, connected with the practical works of life (except, indeed, the work of leading others to knowledge)—this section is the sanctuary, as it were, of this spirit, and ought to be guarded with jealous care, and adorned with everything that is beautiful, by those who watch for the welfare of the whole University. We hope and believe, that those who may have in charge the interests of Yale College will not lose sight of this great work of the coming era. It is one which may appropriately follow, or connect itself with, or even make a part of, that which we set forth in our last Article, and without which, as we believe, the glory of the future will be lost.

THIRD ARTICLE.

As we carry forward the discussion of our general subject from the point which we have now reached, we are naturally led to consider next the schools for professional education. The founding of such schools, as we have already intimated, and as is well known to all who are familiar with the history of the institution, was the work of the far-seeing men who had charge of the College in the earlier part of the present century. They displayed great wisdom, not only in their appreciation of the demand for such schools, and in their readiness to meet that demand by establishing them in connection with the collegiate school which they had received from their fathers, but, also, in their selection of men of ability and reputation, who should become instructors in them and should secure for them a successful growth. Very soon after the establishment of these new departments young men, graduates of this and other institutions, began to resort here in considerable numbers for the pursuit of higher studies. With somewhat varying fortunes, and yet, on the whole, with a steady progress, the schools went onward, until they became known almost as widely as the Academical Department itself. They were honored throughout the country. Graduates went forth from them to adorn the several professions both in the neighborhood of the college and in more distant places. By means of their existence and success, Yale passed out of the company of the institutions with which it had been previously numbered, and took its position in a higher rank—a position which it has maintained until now. Our object, however, is not to trace out the history of these professional schools. We desire, especially, to speak of the coming time, and to refer to the past only so far as it may show any want of completeness, or may indicate the way of better working hereafter.

The great error, as it seems to us, which was made at the beginning in regard to these departments of the University, was in leaving them too dependent on the reputation of one or more instructors. It was, indeed, a day of small things fifty years ago, as compared with the present. We are living now almost in a different world from that which our fathers knew. It would have been idle, therefore, to expect of them a foreseeing of all that might be necessary in after years. Especially was theirs a day of small things in respect to the great matter of money. It was only with the utmost difficulty that funds could be raised for the purposes of education. We can scarcely wonder that they shrank from the work of raising them, and endeavored rather to move on, as best they could, in a limited way. It was natural, also, that, as the new schools began to grow in numbers, they should feel that they were going on successfully enough without further aid, and that the professors were accomplishing all that the institution needed. In this way, comparatively little was accomplished in independence of the power and fame of these particular instructors, and the schools rested almost entirely upon them. Their very success had an influence to close the eyes of even the most interested observers to what must afterwards become manifest, and an essential work was left undone. No institution is strong which depends on the life of a single man. It must have an independent life of its own. It must be able to survive in its vigor and energy, no matter what changes may occur in the occupancy of any one of its chairs of instruction. There must be not a mere collection of students attracted by the brilliancy and power of a favorite teacher, but an institution which draws attention to itself by its own fame, and gives to all who come to it the best education. Yale College, as a college, has always had this essential element of continued success and growth, but, in the earlier times, we think its guardians neglected this point too much in the other departments. And the consequence was, that the work, which was thus passed over at the beginning, became a matter of greater seriousness and difficulty at a later period. New men were obliged to do what their predecessors had failed to do, and to lay foundations, when they ought to have been only building the superstructure.

Another point, in which it seems to us that those who preceded us, (notwithstanding all they accomplished,) made an unfortunate error, was this; that they did not, at the very first moment when they perceived that any of these departments began to decline in strength, make the most strenuous efforts to repair the original error. They should have made the life of the schools as entirely independent as possible of the life of *any* instructor, so soon as they saw them failing, in any measure, because of the passing away of the life of *one* instructor. They should have increased the funds—the essential means of success—as soon as they perceived the first manifestations of weakness arising from the want of funds. But, unfortunately, they did not do this. Unfortunately, we say—for, while it is a manifest fact of the past history, we do not allude to it here with any other intention than to make it helpful or suggestive with regard to the future. The Theological Department of the University, for example, after more than thirty years of its history had elapsed, had only about sixty thousand dollars of available funds—a sum as inadequate to the carrying forward of its work as can well be imagined. Years of effort have been expended, since that time, to bring it, in this regard, even to its present condition, in which it is ready for future and indefinite growth. We do not say that the work could certainly have been done earlier, but no one can doubt that, if it had been done, or if it had been even begun, ten or twenty years before, the result would have been incalculably beneficial. The same thing is true—perhaps in a still greater degree—with regard to some of the other departments. They suffered because they were not strengthened at the critical moment, and thus their growth was arrested for a time, when it might have been uninterrupted and constant.

But, though there may have been unfavorable circumstances or, even, unfortunate mistakes, the University has never lost any part of its organization and never taken a step backward beyond recall. The professional schools have not been abandoned, nor has any such thought been entertained for a moment. On the other hand, the governing powers have been ready to strengthen them and to infuse new life into them whenever the necessity for doing so has become imperative. In the case of some of them, success has been already regained, and enough has been done to show that they may be more vigorous in the future than they have ever been in the past. It becomes a question of great interest, therefore, as we look out upon the coming time, what may be accomplished and what may be hoped for in regard to these schools. If this University can be as prominent and worthy of honor in all its branches, as it now is in its collegiate department, it will hold, always hereafter, a place in the very front rank. If it dies away, in those portions of it where the higher studies are pursued, it must, as we have already pointed out in a former Article, sink into a lower and less influential position. What is the work and what are the thoughts appropriate to the important moment of the College history which is now upon us?

The first feeling, which, as we think, the authorities of the institution, who will have its interests in charge in the period now about to open, ought to fix firmly in their minds, is one of *encouragement.* Yale College and its governors have never been hopeful enough for the last fifty years. The time for a complete change, in this regard, has now arrived. There is every reason, to-day, for confidence in the future, provided only the requisite energy comes forward to meet the crisis. The passing and groundless notion, that a large city or some place other than a University town is best adapted to professional study, is not to be looked upon as likely to keep possession of the minds of the people. When time has been afforded for the mature consideration of the subject in all its bearings, the wise judgment of mankind will decide that the student can most successfully pursue any branch of study at a seat of universal learning. There he is in the atmosphere of study. There he is surrounded by hundreds of earnest and aspiring men who are fired by the noble impulses of the scholar's life, and by their enthusiasm he will be incited to greater energy. There, also, he will be protected against the narrowing influences of his own limited field of working, and will be enlarged in his mental culture, as he sees something of the glory of other fields beyond his own. It is idle, as it seems to us, to endeavor to maintain the opposite view. The "modern American idea," as it is called, that a man ought to know only one thing, lest he should become less practical and effective in that one, or that three-fourths of valuable education consists in "seeing the world" in a great commercial metropolis, is destined to pass away, like other ideas of the same class, so soon as we become a more cultivated people. The study of men is very good in its place, but it is comparatively worthless for the student when it draws him away from books. Books are what he needs in his course of preparation. Mental culture is the thing to which he should give his almost exclusive attention. The knowledge of mankind belongs far more to a later period of life, and it is much more important that a young man should know something, as he enters upon the active duties of his profession, which he can communicate to his fellow-men or with which he can benefit them, than that he should know them themselves thoroughly at the beginning. And—rapidly as we move in this country—it cannot be long before this conviction becomes established everywhere. No doubt, what we say holds good in respect to some professional studies more truly than with reference to others. But, in the case of all alike, they are best pursued where all the circumstances are most favorable to a student's life. Sound learning is the indispensable condition of real power. It ought to be, and, as we believe, will be hereafter, essential to real success. The practical element may be added, but the scholarly element must lie at the foundation. Now the University is the home of learning, and the place where the university is located is, thus, the place for students of every class. So soon as this better judgment becomes established, the attention of men will be turned more fully towards these great institutions. They will be built up in numbers and in strength, while the highest education will be centered in them as much as it now is in Germany. Every advance which is made in right ideas will, thus, become a means of growth for our leading universities, and those among them which are ready to move forward with all energy will be most successful. The outlook upon the future is a bright one. There is no cause for discouragement or doubt.

We add, as a further ground of hopefulness respecting the professional schools of this institution, *the good will* which is very widely entertained towards them. To the Theological Department we have already referred. By a remarkable ordering of Providence, the men who were its earliest officers of instruction continued as fellow-laborers for more than a generation, and then passed off the stage of action almost at the same time. An entirely new organization was, thus, rendered necessary. The funds of the department, however, were so exceedingly limited that but little could be accomplished. For two or three years, the chairs of instruction were only very partially filled, and, then, the breaking out of the late war rendered the collection of the necessary endowments, for the time, impossible. But, with all the weakness of the new beginning, and notwithstanding the many sources of discouragement, the work of reëstablishing and strengthening the school was pressed steadily forward. In the darker times and the brighter times alike, the energies of all interested in it have been constantly exerted for the accomplishment of the end in view. The institution has been made stronger, in some respects, than it ever had been in its earlier history. It has become possessed of a more independent life, and is less a mere assemblage of students about a single eminent man. Its funds have been multiplied seven or eight times. A new building has been erected and completely furnished for the accommodation of its students—one of the largest and most convenient college buildings in the country. Its chairs of instruction are now filled and its number of students is increasing. To those who look back over the past thirteen years, with an intimate knowledge of all that has been accomplished during that period, it is evident that the good will of good men towards Yale College, in any of its departments, may always be depended upon. And, though this particular branch of the University is still in great need of an enlargement of its means, in order that it may fully realize the hopes of its friends and the possibilities of its usefulness, yet those who have its interests in their keeping have greater confidence—and they have reason for greater confidence—that the remaining work can now be done than they have had, heretofore, that any portion of the past results would ever be realized. We allude to this instance only by way of illustration. The remarkable growth and prosperity of the Scientific School—the success which its officers are meeting, even now, in their work of raising a quarter of a million of dollars for its uses—afford another instance of the same thing. The friends of Yale College, and those who believe in and hope for its success, abound everywhere. They will not be slow to help it, in its onward progress, whenever they shall be made to know its wants. They will help its professional schools as well as its collegiate department, and will rejoice in the growth of the former as truly as in that of the latter. If we mistake not the lesson which the past ten years have been reading to the guardians of this university, it has been, first and foremost, the lesson of confidence and hopefulness, in every line.

But there must be *a heroic energy* corresponding to the hopefulness, or the end will not be attained. If the hope can be awakened as it should be, indeed, the energy will naturally follow—and yet, as our second thought, we desire to call attention to the imperative need of the latter. There are professional schools in this University which, at the present moment, are almost entirely destitute of funds. They have struggled on against this evil, as best they could, for years past, and have accomplished results most honorable to themselves. Indeed, there is nothing in the history of Yale College more remarkable, than the greatness of its work when compared with the smallness of its means. But the period in the history of the country has now arrived when such things can be no longer anticipated. With the increased wealth of the nation, it has become essential, that the higher educational institutions should have greatly enlarged endowments. Sooner or later, those which are limited, in this regard, must lose efficiency and fall behind in their work. An effort, as it seems to us, must, therefore, at once be made for the supply of this want in the professional schools here, if the end which we have in view is to be accomplished. And this effort must be directed in a wise way and must be of a most persistent character.

If we consider the condition of the two departments which have been alluded to, when we were speaking of the hopefulness of the future—namely, the Theological and the Scientific—a very large increase of the existing funds is demanded, notwithstanding all that has recently been obtained. Not more, we suppose, than one half of the amount, which the officers of the latter have set before themselves as the smallest sum at which they should aim, has as yet been secured. But these gentlemen have shown such enterprise and earnestness in their work, during the past eighteen months, as to give promise of their ultimate success, and they present an example, in this regard, which may well be imitated. In the former of these two departments, there remains very much to be done. The means for erecting a large addition to its present building, for giving further aid to those among its students who are in pecuniary need, and for increasing the salaries of its instructors, as well as for other purposes, are still to be raised. We know of no reason why the former of these schools may not have, at an early day, two hundred and fifty students, and the latter one hundred or more, except it be from the want of such larger means. Everything else looks favorable, at the present moment, for their prosperous growth; and, though we prophesy nothing, we say, with confidence, that, if the necessary energy in this one line is displayed by the University authorities, these two schools may be placed very soon beyond all danger of declining hereafter. They may become so strong, that the whole University shall rise in power and eminence by means of them. Will the energy and effort that are called for be ready to meet the call? Will the Trustees of the College and all the officers of these schools be prepared for the crisis and the work? Surely, if the work can be accomplished, it will be an occasion of rejoicing among all the friends of the College throughout the country. The University will appear to be growing, not in one department only, but in a well-rounded and healthful way. But the results which have already been realized in the Scientific and Theological schools, in the particular regard of which we are now speaking,—incomplete as they have hitherto been,—are not yet reached in the other professional departments. The Law and Medical schools are nearly destitute of funds. They are dependent, almost entirely, on the fees derived from the students connected with them. The resources of the former are not sufficient to command the services of eminent men, of large and long-continued experience in the profession, as occupants of the principal chairs of instruction, while, in both alike, every teacher is compelled to obtain a considerable, or even the main, portion of his support from his labors outside of the school. How can institutions, which remain in such a condition in these days, hope to grow? How can they accomplish for the University that which they need to accomplish, if the University is to be what it ought to be? We are drawing near, now, to a new era in the history of the institution. One of the most urgent duties of the central authorities at the opening of this era, as it appears to us, is to take hold of this most important matter. The Medical and Law Departments should be placed on firm pecuniary foundations. They should be provided with the necessary means for doing the large work of which they are capable, and for which they are designed. But how is this end to be attained? Not, as we think, by the appointment of an ordinary financial agent. Agents for purposes of this sort are sometimes successful, but they are recognized always as persons who make their living by the business, and their applications are easily rejected, even by the most generous of men. When we say all of them that can, by any means, be said, they cannot speak, in a case like this, with the influence and power which belong to the officers and governors of the whole University. Nor, again, can the results be secured by resolutions setting forth the importance of the object. The work must be undertaken as a business, which is to occupy much thought and is to be extended over any amount of time that may prove to be required. It must be borne in mind, that, in some respects, the undertaking will be more difficult than those which have been partially successful in the other schools. The religious sentiment of the community is always easily awakened to interest in the education of ministers, and the beneficial influence of scientific knowledge in the fields of popular enterprise is now drawing very kindly attention, on the part of large numbers of wealthy men, to the schools of science. But the greater difficulty is to be met by greater determination to overcome it. There is no field, as we believe, in which patient working will be more certainly rewarded, notwithstanding all delays or discouragements, than that of soliciting from benevolent men the means of carrying forward good and useful enterprises. The end, it must be remembered, is, in this case, a most important one for the whole University. It is one for which, as yet, comparatively little effort has been put forth. It is one which calls for great energy and wisdom. The case, therefore, justifies and demands the special intervention of the governing body, and we cannot but feel that the chief officer of the institution at the commencement of the new era should take upon himself the leading part in the work. He can speak with authority and with influence by reason of his very position. The men of wealth and standing and benevolent feeling in every profession and in every part of the State will gladly meet him, and coöperate with him in any good work for the University. His presence in the enterprise will give unity and efficiency to it, and his encouragement and sympathy will be of the greatest assistance to all who are engaged in carrying it forward. Whatever may be his duty, or may be best for him as the presiding official, in ordinary cases, *there is here an emergency which requires his personal effort.* He must be the leader whom others are to follow. The Faculties of these schools must find themselves supported by him and incited to continual earnestness by what they see in him. It is a groundless fear, as we believe, to doubt any longer the possibility of success in such an undertaking. Such fears may have had some foundation, or at least, some seeming foundation, until now. The period of large giving has but recently begun, while the necessities of the times have suddenly enlarged themselves above all former conceptions. But the turning point has now come, beyond which there should be no more apprehension, except, indeed, what may be needful for the incitement of constant energy. We earnestly hope, that, before another collegiate year shall have passed away, a beginning may be made—a beginning which shall know no ending but that of complete success. The ending cannot be reached in a year—perhaps, not in ten years—but the result is worth all the effort it will cost, and the success will begin early enough to reward and encourage the earnest worker.

We have dwelt at some length and, perchance, with some degree of repetition, in this and former Articles, on this subject of the necessity of immediate effort for the increase of the funds of the institution. We shall be compelled to refer to it again hereafter. It is at this point, that one of the greatest needs, and perhaps the very greatest need, of each and all the departments of the University is found. Means of instruction, apparatus, libraries, buildings, even the men themselves who give life and power to the institution, are all secured or lost according to the provision which is made in this regard. At the same time, the work of continually increasing such funds is so laborious, and so unattractive to most men, that they are ever ready to relax their energies. The impelling influences of every new crisis, as it comes, therefore, and the indispensable necessity of accomplishing the end, need to be brought forward with all emphasis, if we are to discuss the future of the College at all. But with reference to the professional schools—and, especially, those to which we have made particular allusion—it would scarcely be possible to say anything, unless we were to draw attention to this fundamental point. In our first Article, we suggested that a combined effort should be made for all branches of the institution together. The work of which we now speak, might be connected with that greater one: and if the greater one is undertaken, as we hope it may be, these schools, which are most needy, should be allowed not only the results of the more special effort made in their behalf, but, also, their appropriate share of what may be obtained for the common good. One of the very first and most essential of all the steps to be taken, when the new era begins, is that which will secure to these schools, that are now so limited in their resources, the means of doing their work—the foundation in respect to their funds, which will enable them to be, in their appropriate sphere, what the Academical Department already is in its own.

If we turn from the consideration of the need of enlarged funds, in regard to which the professional schools are essentially alike, to inquire respecting some of their other wants for the coming time, we shall find it necessary to speak of them more individually. The Law Department is, at present, in a peculiar condition. Its leading professor, who for many years had a principal part, and, recently, almost the whole of the work of instruction under his charge, was called away by death two years ago. As the endowments were very limited, it was found impracticable to make new appointments as fully as could have been desired, and a provisional and temporary arrangement was made, by which the department passed under the care of three members of the bar in New Haven. It was hoped, at the time when they undertook the charge of the school, that, at no very remote day, their work might, at least, be supplemented by the election of one or more professors. This end, however, has not as yet been accomplished. The reorganization of the school is, therefore, still incomplete, and must be regarded as, in a very special sense, belonging to the new era. In some of the other departments, the work of the future is only a partial one. The past ten or fifteen years have secured certain results which are fixed and permanent. From these they can go forward, as from a starting point for new efforts. But, here, the beginning only has been made. If the old life and vigor are again to be restored, almost everything is yet to be done. It may not belong to one who is outside of the range of legal studies, to suggest what course of action should be adopted in this matter. We should, certainly, feel ourselves incapable of setting forth the whole subject with any degree of fullness. But we may offer one or two thoughts, as we trust without impropriety, which will meet the approval of all who believe, as we do, that the several parts of the University must increase together, hereafter, if the University itself is to have any proper and noble life. At the earliest possible moment,—as soon as the necessary endowments shall have been secured, or even before they are fully secured—one or more of the professorships should be filled with men of years and eminence and attractive power as teachers. The true organization for every institution of learning of the higher class, whether college or professional school, is, doubtless, that which combines the instructions and energies of younger men with those of men who are older. Where such institutions are to be strengthened for a new work, the hopefulness and enthusiasm of young men are absolutely essential. Men who are drawing near the end of life are, generally, deficient in these qualities. They are, almost always, unfitted for those constant efforts which are demanded under such circumstances. But those who are still comparatively young have the heroism of youth, and hard and uninterrupted labor for a future reward is what they are prepared to meet, and what they even rejoice in. Yet, on the other hand, they alone are not sufficient. They are rarely possessed of that wide-spread reputation which is needful for the fame of the institution, and of which students at a distance think so much. If the two orders of instructors could be combined here, in the new arrangements of this school, the first great step in the desired progress would be taken. It cannot be taken, indeed, unless previous efforts shall have been made for the securing of the endowments of which we have spoken, but we have no evidence, as yet, that those efforts cannot be made successfully at an early day.

In the appointments of such new officers, and as it seems to us, in the raising of such funds, the governors of the University should not deliberate among themselves or with persons in New Haven alone. They should call into their counsels gentlemen of wisdom from the graduates who are engaged in this profession in other cities and in other states, and should open before them a large and comprehensive plan, which should be worthy of the University and should be calculated, for this very reason, to interest their minds. There are friends of the College, also, outside of the legal profession and outside of the number of the graduates, who would give valuable aid and advice, if asked to do so. These persons might well be consulted. Some of them—even in cases where no one had supposed them likely to be interested in this particular department—might become contributors to its prosperity. Very few of them, as we are persuaded, would fail to give encouragement, and thus, new strength for the prosecution of the work. The governing board are unable to perform this duty by themselves in the wisest manner. It is a case where they peculiarly need assistance from others—and, while they should originate the plan and determine to carry it forward to success, they should not attempt the accomplishment of the work, or even the full maturing of the plan, except in concert with men to whom, in some respects, the things essential to the end in view are more thoroughly known.

We may add, in this connection, another suggestion, which may be regarded as of some importance. This department of the University, during a portion of its past history, has suffered in no inconsiderable degree from the fact, that its instructors have been too busily engaged in the practice of their profession. They have, thus, been divided in their thoughts and labors, and have not been able to devote themselves exclusively to the interests of the school. This condition of things has not, indeed, been altogether a matter of their own choice, but a certain necessity has been laid upon them; yet of the unfavorable effect of it we have had testimony, in past times, from those who were best capable of judging. Now, in the future, we think an effort should be made to remedy this evil. If professors should be appointed who should give their time and energies as entirely to the work of instruction, as those do who are in the Academical and Scientific departments, the prospects of the school would at once be brightened. In our judgment, the former professors fell into an error in this respect. Not, indeed, that they could entirely have escaped the necessity to which we have just alluded, but if they had broken away from it as much as possible, they would have strengthened the school so far that the necessity itself—which was one arising from insufficient funds—would gradually have diminished in its force. A teacher needs to be wholly a teacher—not half given up to the work of a laborious profession and only half to his own employment. A man cannot be an active pastor and a professor of Systematic Theology in a Theological Seminary at the same time. No more should he be an active lawyer and a professor of law. At the least, he should mainly be engaged in the duties of his professorship, and they should be the first of all things in his view. If we mistake not, it will be essential to the growth of this department in the future, that, in the new arrangements, provision should be made for such exclusive devotion to its interests and work on the part of those who carry on its instruction. The legal business of these professors must be like the preaching work of their colleagues in the theological school—not a work coördinate with that of their special office, but wholly subordinate to it.

That a new building for the purposes of the Law School, which we suppose might be erected for a moderate sum, and a very large increase of the library will be necessary to the highest success of the institution, are so evident to all who are familiar with its present condition as scarcely to need any mention here. The present building will be inadequate to the wants of the school as soon as its numbers increase, and will not afford it a proper home. Of the importance of books all must be conscious, for this is the profession which, more than any other, perhaps, demands reading within its own field, and the University library is not supplied in this department as well, even, as it is in theology or natural science. But these wants will be supplied so soon as funds are secured for the purpose, and in urging the increase of funds we have, in reality, urged the importance of securing these immediate and natural results of such increase.

The points, which we have now suggested, will hold good, in a considerable measure, with reference to the Medical Department also, though here there is already provided a building sufficient for its present wants. The Medical School, however, differs widely from the Law School in one important respect. Its chairs of instruction are filled, and its officers constitute a body of men who can encourage and strengthen one another in their work far better than those can, who are fewer in number and who feel that some of the important places are still vacant. But if the teachers in the Medical Department could—even a portion of them—be relieved from their pressing employments outside of the school, and so have the opportunity of watching more constantly over its interests, it can scarcely be doubted that great advantages would be secured. We think the aim should be to have—at the earliest practicable day—some men in the institution who shall be wholly given to the science, while others mingle with the scientific the practical element, in their daily work, so that the students can derive the full benefit of both.

There is one unfavorable circumstance in the size of the city where this University is located, as bearing upon the Law and Medical departments, and especially upon the latter. It is that the opportunities for observing and becoming familiar with the practice of the professions are better in the great cities of the country. Especially is this true with regard to the work in hospitals. It may be that this fact may always give larger numbers of students to schools established in those cities. And yet it may be questioned whether—even with regard to these schools—it will not prove, in the long run, that those will be most successful in which the best instruction and the best opportunities of study are given. These, however, are advantages which, as we have already seen, are found in connection with a University, rather than anywhere else. Already, if we are not in error, the plan for medical instruction in the school here, is a more thorough one than has yet been adopted in other places; and, if it is well carried out, it cannot fail to be successful. The day is approaching when the system of cramming students of this science with six lectures a day, following each other in six successive hours, and after two courses of this kind of sixteen weeks' continuance, turning them out upon the world to exercise their art, will meet as universal condemnation as it deserves. But when it does come, those schools will be recognized as worthy of credit and support, where another and more reasonable system has been established, and students will come to them for an education. It must be remembered, also, that New Haven is a rapidly-growing city, and will secure to itself steadily, as it goes forward, the peculiar advantages of larger towns. We believe, therefore, that, with wisdom in the selection of instructors and with proper energy in the carrying forward of the work of the institutions both within and without, these two schools may take and hold a very prominent place in the future, as they, unquestionably, have done in the past.

A peculiarity of the Theological Department, which distinguishes it from all the others, is found in the fact that a very large proportion of its students are limited in their means. Instruction must, therefore, be furnished free of charge, and beneficiary funds must be provided to meet the necessities of the case. The Department needs strengthening at a point, where the other schools can help themselves by reason of fees derived from their pupils. The organization of all our Theological institutions throughout the country has, from the beginning, been arranged with reference to this peculiarity, and we do not see how it can be essentially changed. Indeed, there is a manifest propriety in the present system of things. If the nation educates its military officers at a national academy free of all charge, and supports them while they are in their course of study, and if it does so, not out of charity to them, but because it cannot exist without an educated soldiery, surely the Church ought to do the same thing and for the same reason. A thoroughly educated ministry is a vital necessity to the Christian body. The work of the gospel cannot go forward without it, for it is the divinely appointed means of accomplishing the work. It is by preaching that the world is to be saved. The providing of such a ministry, and the securing for them the best possible preparation for their office, should be looked upon, not as a gift of benevolence to the men who are thus educated, so much as a privilege and duty of the Christian Church. The feeling should be just what the feeling of the nation is, and ought to be, towards the school at West Point. Moreover, as the first and highest duty of the followers of Christ is to extend his kingdom, and as those among them who are possessed of abundant means suffer themselves so generally to be drawn away to other and more lucrative employments,—and the direct work of the ministry is, thus, left mainly to those who are poor—there is an obligation of the most sacred character resting upon the richer portion to aid these who take upon themselves the great work. If the wealthier part of the Church do not themselves assume their share of this responsibility of preaching the gospel, they should see that those who do assume it for them are provided with all needed means of support. The regarding of this matter as a charity is no proper view of it. It is one of the most important duties of the Church. But if the facts and necessities of the case are thus, every institution for theological education must be greatly dependent for its success on the provision of such funds for the assistance of its students. The institution here needs, at the present time, a special effort for this end.

In all these professional schools, as in all departments of the University, the standard of scholarship needs continual advancement. This is a matter of course. It is a work which can never cease, unless the life and power of the University are to die away. Such advancement has characterized the past history, and, as we believe, all those connected with the various schools are earnest in their purpose that it shall, in like manner, characterize the future. In the professional schools, however, even more than in the undergraduate departments, it is important, to this end, that the instructors should be men of magnetic and inspiring character. This most desirable power is a rare one among teachers, as among other men, but it ought to be sought for whenever new appointments are to be made, and every instructor now engaged in his work should cultivate it to the utmost possible extent. We have spoken of it as even peculiarly important in the professional departments, for, in addition to the attractive influence which it gives, it supplies one of the great needs of professional education. The work of the Academical Department is, much more entirely, in the line of drill and mere mental exercise and discipline. It is, also, much more complete within its own limits. But professional education is a thing of a life-time, and the school devoted to it only opens the door to the life-long work. The inspiration of enthusiasm must, therefore, be given to the student at the outset, that he may have, afterward, when he comes to be separated from outward helps, a self-propelling force within himself. The instructor who can impart such enthusiasm, inciting the minds of all who come under his teaching to an earnest and unquenchable desire for learning, has accomplished a result which is of greater moment than almost any other that can be thought of. It must not, indeed, be an enthusiasm for the instructor's own system. The inspiring power loses half its value, or perhaps the whole of it, when this is the end. But it must be an ardent love of learning and truth, in the particular line of study in which he is leading forward his classes. We believe that this object can be accomplished more easily in a University than anywhere else, because there the atmosphere of learning is on every side of the student, and the enthusiasms from every department readily concentrate their influences on each individual mind.

In regard to the Scientific School, which, in its higher section, belongs with the professional departments, there are one or two peculiar needs which may, with propriety, be alluded to in this connection. This department, from the character of the field which it occupies, requires a much more numerous body of professors than any of the other three which have been mentioned. Provision is, therefore, continually needed for new chairs of instruction, as the subjects of consideration in natural science extend themselves more widely and deeply. The Faculty of Science, if it be full, must, almost of necessity, be the largest Faculty of the University. At the same time, the wants of this department in the line of apparatus and means of investigation are such as, from the nature of the case, know scarcely any limits. We cannot but feel, also, that the Scientific School of this University needs one or more buildings for the accommodation of its graduate or professional as well as its undergraduate students. The question of the desirableness of college buildings, where young men may find their homes during the years of their education, is a question much debated by the public. It is one in regard to which, at present, the advantages of both sides are being tried at Yale College—the Academical Department being provided with such buildings, while the Scientific Department has, as yet, made no special effort to secure them. Perhaps, this is the wisest course to be followed for a few years to come, until a more perfect and satisfactory trial shall have led to a decision in which all can agree. But the reasons in favor of such buildings, which arise from the friendly associations and the academic *esprit de corps* which they tend to develop, and, even, from the economy of expense which they occasion, will, finally, as it seems to us, overbalance all things which can be urged upon the other side. If a building, or more than one if needed, were open for the students of the Scientific School, we are assured, from facts which have come to our own knowledge, that numbers of young men, who are now much pressed to meet their expenses, or who are prevented from entering the school, would find the way of their education made much plainer and smoother. The munificence of one of the liberal and large-minded citizens of New Haven has provided this department with a building well adapted for its public purposes. If others in the city, or the state, should be moved to erect another building, for the purpose which we have indicated, it would be of great advantage to the department, and, through it, to the whole University. We do not, however, press this point with the same urgency, with which we insist upon the others previously mentioned, because we suppose many of the officers of this school are still doubtful respecting its importance.

We have not attempted to present all the wants of these various schools. Many of them are thoroughly understood by those alone who are constantly engaged in their service. Our only design is to set forth some of the more special and leading ones among them. That the opening of the new era, which is now close upon us, is the most favorable time for entering upon the work of supplying these wants, can scarcely be doubted. Every new crisis in the history of such an institution is a time of peculiar possibilities and peculiar hopefulness. The interest of its friends centers upon it, with a new energy, because it is starting afresh for a further and higher progress. A work can be done, at such a time, which might have been beyond the possibilities of an earlier period, and may, even, prove to be far more difficult in a future one. If there is delay or half-heartedness, until it has passed, no one can estimate the measure of the loss. But if heroic earnestness and unselfish devotion seize upon the critical moment, everything will prove helpful to the accomplishment of the end. There are large numbers of persons, as we believe—persons whose love for Yale College is as warm as could be desired, and whose interest in the College must be one of the chief supports on which it is to rest in the coming years—who desire to see a strong University here. They are graduates of the Academical Department, most of them, and they count it one of the great blessings of their life that they are so. They hope, and trust that this Department—the old College, where the four happiest years of youth were spent—may grow in strength continually, and may number, ere long, a thousand students in its classes. But they wish to see the other departments increasing, also, and becoming, in the most complete sense, coördinate members of one great institution. They believe this change from the College with loosely-attached outside schools into the well-rounded and harmoniously-developed University to be the one all-important work of the opening era. Whatever favors the accomplishment of this result they hail with satisfaction. Whatever opposes it they grieve over as a sign of coming evil. It is with the sympathy of all this goodly company, we are sure, that we write; and, for the end which in common with them we desire, we press the importance of building up, in every way, those departments of the University where the higher and professional studies are provided for. When they have been thus strengthened, their life will react for its highest well-being upon the collegiate department, and the success as well as the fame of the whole institution will be greater than it can be otherwise.

FOURTH ARTICLE.

The work of the new era in the undergraduate departments of the University is the subject which will occupy our attention in the present Article. Of these departments, the one which is connected with the Scientific School is of recent growth, and has some of the peculiar wants to which we have referred in connection with the schools for professional study. The other is the original College, established at the beginning of the last century, and strong with the power and fame of its past history. It needs larger development, indeed, and a progress fitted to the coming times, but it is secure in its position as one of the two leading collegiate institutions of the country. The claim of the guardians and friends of Yale College is, that, by the establishment of these two departments, side by side, the most satisfactory arrangement possible has been made both for the classical and the scientific methods of education. The great question between the old and the new systems, as they are sometimes called, which is now agitating the public mind, is one that cannot be wisely settled until after the excitement of the first onset and struggle shall have passed away. The interests of sound learning, at the present moment and while the discussion is going forward, demand, first of all, that the two systems be so placed in contrast with each other, that they may show their own especial excellences and defects. If they are intermingled with one another, or the students, who are pursuing the different lines of study, are brought together in the same classes or the same institution, this end cannot be successfully attained. In most other colleges this is the course adopted. But here the work in either line is unmingled with and unhindered by that in the other. Each system has full opportunity to develop itself and to do all that it can do in its own way. We believe that the officers of this University in all its departments are alike of the opinion, that our method of adjusting this matter is the best one. The experience of the years since it was adopted has only confirmed this opinion, and the steady growth of both the classical and scientific schools bears witness that the public sentiment outside of the college is not out of harmony with the views which are entertained here. It would seem, indeed, that these views must be founded in reason and must, therefore, be in accordance with truth; for the decision of this most important question must depend, in the final result, on the feeling and consciousness, if we may so say, of the individual student. If the man who is classically educated feels and knows within himself, that he stands on a higher level of intellectual cultivation than his associate who has followed the new education, and if this associate knows and feels that he is himself on a lower grade,—if this is true of every fair-minded student in either line, or of the great majority of such students, the determination will, ere long, be reached by the public mind, that the old is better than the new. If, on the other hand, the opposite state of things shall prove to be true, the opposite decision will be accepted as the final one. But the two students must stand apart in their education, and the institutions for the different studies must be side by side and not be mingled in one, if the comparison, which is essential to the end in view, is to be properly made. For ourselves, we believe that the settlement of this question will rest upon certain unchangeable facts—which are lost sight of now, because we are at the most unfavorable point of the controversy for the calmness of consideration and wise judgment—and that, if we can give the opportunity for such individual comparison as we have spoken of above, there will be little occasion to apprehend the result. It is a part of the wisdom of the managers of Yale College, that they have, so carefully and thoroughly, provided such an opportunity.

But our object is not to discuss the merits of the two systems, or even to set forth, at length, any peculiar excellence of this University with respect to the adjustment between them. Whether wisely or not, the decision here has been made to carry forward the different lines of study in different departments of the institution, and we may presume that the unanimous judgment of the officers of both the departments will not easily be altered. We may accept it, therefore, as a settled point, that the opening era is not to change the order of things in regard to these fundamental arrangements, but that its work is to be that of enlarging and developing both the separate branches. How should *this* work be carried forward is the question of greatest interest, at the present moment, and the question on which we propose to present a few suggestions to our readers.

In respect to the Academical Department the coming years will call for progress, as we think, both in the provisions made for instruction and in the methods of teaching. If we may refer to these two points in their order, we suppose that, among the changes in the arrangements for instruction, none is more generally demanded by thoughtful friends of the College than the partial or complete abolition of the Tutorial office. In this institution, at present, about one half of the education of the students is committed to those holding this office. These persons are young men, who have been graduated two or three years, and who are purposing, after a brief period of teaching, to enter upon some other work in life. They are, commonly, men of good scholarship and possessed of some degree of that genuine enthusiasm which belongs to their age, but, owing either to the method of choosing them or to unavoidable circumstances, they are not very unfrequently of limited capabilities or qualifications as teachers. By reason of some fault in the system, also, they are not always assigned to that particular department of instruction for which they are, by their tastes or their acquisitions, best fitted, but the man whose inclinations and studies have been in the line of mathematics is obliged, for a time at least, to become the guide of his pupils in Latin or Greek. For these reasons and others which might be named, almost all persons who now graduate at this college have, as we believe, at the time of their graduation and afterward, grave doubts about the whole Tutorial system. The advocates of the system are largely among the older men, who do not easily escape the influences under which they grew up, in their earlier years. For ourselves, we do not think that this office ought to be entirely given up. The continual infusion of new blood into a college faculty is a health-giving thing. Young men, too, are apt to be more ready to teach the rudimentary parts of studies and to be more enthusiastic for this work, than those who have, in their own progress, gone far beyond the beginnings and have been teachers of successive classes for many years. The Freshmen and Sophomores in our colleges, so long as the preparatory schools do not advance far beyond their present state, must be employed with these rudiments. They are boys in their intellectual development, and they must be taught as boys. In general, the work which they need can be well done by those who, but a few years ago, were in their own condition, and who not only remember, but are interested in, what they are now studying. Older men are often wearied with these things because they are older. They have risen to the higher regions of learning and are interested there. Moreover, in institutions like our American colleges, where the students are to be governed, and the Faculty, as it is often said, stand in the place of parents, it is of great importance that a portion of the governing power should have recently come from the student community. The young man of 1820 or 1830 was, in many respects, different and widely different from his successor in 1870. The instructor, therefore, who finished his student life forty years ago, does not, in all points, understand the feelings and sentiments of the undergraduate of to-day. He does not—so strange is the influence of the passing years—even remember his own sentiments and feelings as they were in the distant past. There seems, oftentimes, to be an almost impassable barrier between the older officers and their pupils, in this regard, which wholly prevents the former from properly appreciating the peculiarities of the latter; and, whenever such is the fact, the government is likely to be administered more or less unwisely. We believe that the Tutors in Yale College have always done their full share in the work, not only of discipline, but of reasonable discipline on the part of the governing body, and that they have, very frequently, by reason of their more thorough understanding of the present interior life of the college community, arrested mistaken measures and corrected erroneous views. Students, in general, are not ready to do them justice, because they seem but little older than themselves. But, so far as our observation has extended, we are sure that they have been of great service to the institution, and have constituted an element in the college which could not well be dispensed with.

But, while we admit and maintain all this, we do not see how it can well be doubted, that the Tutors here are too large a part of the Academical Faculty. Permanent instructors, devoting their lives to their several branches of study, are what a collegiate institution most needs. Young men who have made but little progress, and who are intending soon to enter upon one of the three learned professions, are not qualified to do so large a portion of the whole academic teaching. They do not know enough. They are not concentrated sufficiently in their purposes upon this one work. They are ordinarily obliged to give a considerable share of their time and efforts to other studies, in preparation for their future business. With their time divided and their thoughts drawn in different ways, they lose efficiency and sometimes slight their college duties. They are instructors whose life, so to speak, is only half within the institution. How can they be as useful as the permanent professors, who are as completely devoted to their work as the lawyer or physician is to his?

The education at Yale College is not inferior to what it is in many other institutions because there are a considerable number of Tutors here,—for, in the first place, the proportion of these officers to the more permanent ones is not larger than in the small colleges where there are fewer of both, and, in the second place, there are many persons in other institutions wearing the title of professors, who are no better qualified for their work than these younger teachers here are. Nor do we see any evidence that Yale College has suffered thus far, in the public estimation, on account of this Tutorial instruction. But it must be remembered that we are now about entering upon a new era, in which scholarship is to be carried forward beyond the limits which it has already reached. A community of scholars is growing up in the country, who will both elevate and guide public opinion in this matter. More will be demanded of our colleges than has yet been asked for, and, if the demands which are reasonable are not met by any institution, that institution will so far fail of future success. An imperative necessity resting upon the Academical Department of this University will require, in the early future, as we cannot doubt, the substitution of professorships for most of our tutorships, and the abandonment, thus, in large measure, of the old system of the past. The occupants of the Tutorial office, so far as that office shall still remain, will need to be chosen in some different way, and for a longer period, than has hitherto been the case. They will need to be men who are preparing for the teacher's rather than the minister's or lawyer's work, and who, for this reason, are able and willing to give their whole energies to their office. They will need, also, to be assigned to their duties only on the ground of their fitness, and not according to the rule that the oldest in office is to have the choice of departments. In our second Article was suggested, as we believe, one of the best ways of selecting not only the Tutors but, also, almost all the officers of instruction for the college—namely, the method of selecting them from the company of those graduated students who shall be pursuing higher and non-professional studies at the University itself. In this way, every such student will have the greatest stimulus to make the utmost progress possible, and the governing powers of the institution will have the most abundant, as well as the best, opportunities to observe the capacities and adaptations of the candidates for office. The time is rapidly coming, if, indeed, it has not already come, when our largest Universities must educate their own instructors for their work, and when they can no longer content themselves with the services, for two or three years, of young men who are designing to live in some other sphere, but must secure for a lifetime the men of greatest ability and of highest enthusiasm.

Another demand of the coming epoch will be the increase of the number of instructors. This demand, indeed, is a constant one in every growing institution of learning, and has been felt here in the past as truly as it will be. We have now, however, arrived at a period when decided and marked advancement must be made, or the College will be in danger of falling back. The graduates and friends of the Academical Department ought carefully to consider its wants in this direction, and, if they would make it worthy of the age, they should provide the means for the establishment of these new chairs of instruction. Especially in the departments of English Literature, of Latin, and of the Modern Languages, as well as in Astronomy and International Law, additional professors should be appointed at the earliest possible day. But our object in alluding to this point is not to repeat what has been pressed upon the public attention, more than once of late, by others, but to suggest that necessity of an increased number of instructors which arises from the very large and increasing number of students. When the College classes have reached the number of one hundred and fifty or more, they cannot be taught successfully by three or four persons, as they could be when consisting of seventy or eighty only. Indeed, we regard it as having been, for more than twenty five years, one of the misfortunes of Yale College, that its teachers have been so few. A division of thirty students is too large to recite together with the highest advantage. Where instruction is given largely by lectures, as is the case in the professional schools to a great extent, this remark will not hold good. But, in the Academical Department, the main work is and ought to be in the line of recitations, and, under such circumstances, fifteen or twenty are as many as should meet together. The larger number prevents all familiarity and spontaneity in the exercise. It limits, of necessity, the instruction to simple questioning on the part of the teacher and answering on that of the pupil, and, thus, quenches or, at least, fails to excite the enthusiasm of the student. Large colleges are more advantageous than small ones in so many ways, that there can be no doubt that it is best for any man, who is able to do so, to go to them. But, *in this respect*, they are attended by a disadvantage, unless the teachers are made more numerous in proportion to the number of pupils.

We have mentioned these two requirements which are now pressing upon us, because they are felt, in their importance, so generally by that class of persons who, like ourselves, believe in the desirableness of forwarding the growth of a University in this place. They may well be mentioned, also, because they will have a direct tendency towards making the University what it ought to be, by advancing and fostering scholarly enthusiasm in that Department which is at the foundation, as it were, of the other and higher schools.

If we turn, now, to consider the methods of teaching, we may be led, incidentally, to refer to some other demands of the new era, and, thus, in some measure, to complete what must, from the limits imposed upon us, be necessarily an imperfect exposition of the wants of the Department. Much has been written, of late, in the way of complaint respecting the mode of instruction in this college, and, especially, with reference to the want of any enthusiastic love of study among the undergraduate students, which want, it is claimed, is due to the system of teaching. We have every reason to believe and to know, that the same complaints may be made as justly against all American Colleges, but the charge is, doubtless, intended to bear upon all alike, although, for special reasons, it is now brought forward by many against this one alone. The charge of want of enthusiasm among students is one which we acknowledge to be true. There are, as we are persuaded, comparatively few young men in our collegiate institutions, who are fired with any unquenchable love for the studies in which they are engaged. Enthusiasm comes, to some extent, after men have completed their undergraduate course and have entered upon their professional studies or upon their life-work, but, with now and then an exception, it does not inspire those who are at the earlier stage. It ought, however, to be remembered by persons who make the complaint, that the fact is largely owing to the simple reason of their being at the early stage. Boys do not love to study, as a general thing. Unless they are remarkable boys, or unless they have very remarkable teachers, they begin the course of learning rather under the influence of necessity than of love. Nor is this true of their beginnings in *learning only*. The same fact is observable in every other work. Indeed, nothing characterizes the great mass of men, in mature life, more than the want of that inspiration which is connected with genuine ardor in their pursuits. The necessity laid upon us all is the motive without which we should be in danger of neglecting our business, and it would be strange if it were not even more so with the young. Many seem to suppose that, if the compulsory attendance upon lectures and recitations could be given up, and what is called the marking system abandoned, the evils of the present would, at once, disappear and a kind of golden age begin. But our observation of human nature, as exhibited in any institution of learning which we have seen either in this country or in Europe, does not encourage us to look for any such result. In fact, our experience in connection with one or two of the German Universities, a few years ago, where the students are at a higher point of education than our undergraduates, and are, therefore, more capable of being trusted with freedom from rules, has convinced us of the necessity of the compulsory system, so far as its essential features are concerned. A body of youth, just passing from boyhood to manhood, who are left at liberty to attend or not, as they please, the exercises of a college, are likely to be not only a body of idlers but an intolerable evil in a community. Perhaps the marking system may be modified, or something in the way of frequent examinations, as bearing upon success, may be substituted for it, but the fundamental element in this system —namely, the honoring of students according to their rank and faithfulness—is no hindrance to enthusiasm, and is only a legitimate application of the principle of rewarding those who deserve it. That there is something in the compulsory method which, because it drives rather than draws, hinders the growth of love for his studies in the student's mind, we think is undoubtedly true. But we regard this method as a necessity because of the evils unavoidably resulting from its abolition; and the hindrance of which we have spoken is only a small one in comparison with others that will exist whether it is rejected or retained. The question for our American Colleges, then, as it seems to us, is not the question as to a fundamental and radical change in this respect, but it is the question how enthusiasm in study—that most desirable of all objects—may be awakened under the present organization of things. We believe that it can be, and ought to be, thus awakened to a far greater extent than it has been. In our second Article, we were led, incidentally, to suggest two or three points of great importance in connection with this matter. It will be unnecessary to dwell upon them again in this place, but it seems to us that, first of all things, provision needs to be made for that greater familiarity of communication between the pupil and his instructor in the recitation-room, to which we have alluded. By the adoption of this single change in our present method, one-half, or more than one-half, of the existing evil might be removed. The student may, properly, be obliged to attend the exercises of his class. Indeed, without some sense of responsibility in this regard, he will often waste his time and abuse his privileges. But, when he comes to the exercises, he ought to have free opportunity to question his teacher and to bring forward, in a suitable way, the topics and thoughts which have been interesting his own mind. One of the great reasons why the members of the professional schools are more enthusiastic in their work than college students are, is, doubtless, this larger freedom in the lecture-room. In every well-organized law school or theological seminary, the young men are encouraged to ask for the solution of all their difficulties, and to discuss, within proper bounds, the subjects which are brought before them. The lecture hour is, often, lengthened for this purpose, and the time which follows the close of the formal exercise is, often, more stimulating to enthusiasm than the lecture itself. Probably this course cannot be adopted to the same extent in the undergraduate department, but it can be to a considerable extent, and, so far as it may be adopted, it will be attended with a similar result. Let the divisions of the class be arranged, as they are now in this college, according to the attainments and proficiency of the students, and, then, let them be limited in number to fifteen persons, and who can doubt that a faithful and inspiring teacher can accomplish much in this most desirable line? Individuals will not be compelled, as now, to suffer because of the numbers who are to be examined, and the examination of whom is necessary in order to their faithfulness. But, while time will be given for all necessary questioning on the part of the instructor, there will, also, be opportunity for the student to bring forward the results of his own independent investigation, and, thus, there will be the means of inciting him to such investigation. As we have already seen, however, this change in the present system will require a very considerable increase in the number of teachers. If it is to be accomplished, the friends of the college must enlarge its resources. The opening era calls upon them for large gifts to this end.

Another change, to which allusion was made in the Article referred to, and which, though it might be discussed at greater length, we will only mention again at the present time, is in the method of teaching the classical languages—so that by limiting the instructions less exclusively to the grammar, and by giving more facility in translation and more appreciation of the beauty of style and thought, a more thorough knowledge of the glory of those languages, as well as a deeper love for them, may be produced. Unless something is done to this end, and efficiently done, we fear that the conflict, which is going forward in regard to the use of these languages in education, may turn out disastrously for a time, by reason of the errors of the classical party. Comparatively few students can be made to enjoy grammar, or to love the science of philology. These things belong, like the higher mathematics, within the region of the enthusiasm of a selected company. But almost all students, of respectable ability and faithfulness, may be aroused, as we believe, to read the Greek and Latin poets with pleasure, and to acknowledge the refining influence of these studies upon their own minds. With some, of course, it will be more difficult to accomplish this result than with others, but with the great majority it can be done, if the right method be adopted, and the teacher, gifted with magnetic power, be faithful to his office.

But, without lingering longer upon this point, we urge, in the next place, that our present system involves far too much of memorizing. Verbal memory—the power to commit a passage word for word—is comparatively useless in after life. The thing which a man of education needs, is, to grasp the thoughts and substance of what he reads, for, without this power, he can hardly be a scholar in any profession. Now the former power is the one which is cultivated, almost altogether, in our colleges. Students are even expected or required to learn the lists of words and sentences which illustrate some minute and comparatively unimportant rule in grammar so accurately that they can recite them without any question on the part of the teacher —each one beginning where the preceding student left off in his recitation, and going on until he, in his turn, is allowed to stop. They are expected to recite works in history and, sometimes, even a book like Olmsted's Natural Philosophy, almost verbatim. We believe such memorizing, carried to such an extent, to be not only useless but positively injurious to the mind. If a youth is occupied with learning by rote, from the age of ten to the age of twenty—the formative period of the mind—

he will weaken his memory in those other lines in which it must be of priceless value to him. It is with the deepest regret, and almost with a feeling of indignation, that we recall the baleful influence of some of our early teaching in this regard, and there is a well-known book, the mere mention of which brings to our thought a loss, which we suffered from such memoriter recitations in years gone by, whose greatness is appreciated only the more fully the farther we advance in our course. It is not the object of a man's life in this world, as some one has said, to spend half of his career in getting ready for college and the other half in going through college. If it were, such methods of study might be defended. But college life is valueless except in its bearing on the future, and if college life does not give us what best fits us for the demands of that future and what developes the mind in the way in which it needs to grow, it fails of its only worthy end. It is not the schoolmaster's estimate of the excellence of the recitations of his pupils, which determines the real value of their work under his care. It is what the pupils, in their later life, judge respecting it from their own experience—it is what they see to have been the influence upon their own minds, that decides the question. Estimated according to this standard, we cannot doubt that the coming years will press a demand upon all our collegiate institutions, and upon Yale College among others, for a change in the matter of which we are now speaking. We only add, in this connection, that such verbal memorizing is a hindrance, rather than an incentive, to enthusiasm. The effort of the mind which it requires is a disagreeable one to most persons, and one which never becomes very attractive. It is the thoughts of a book, not its words, which educated minds love to possess themselves of. The method of education which teaches how to grasp the thoughts will be far more sure to stimulate that earnestness in study and devotion to learning for its own sake which are so desirable—and, thus, the evil of which so many now complain will be most successfully removed. Twenty years ago,—we believe that the experience of all the classes will justify us in saying,—the question least thought of by undergraduate students was the question of the course of thought in the book they were translating. In the new era, and long before another twenty years shall have passed, we hope it will be, if not the first, the most interesting and most important of all questions to their minds.

We cannot but feel, again, that, in the coming years, there will be a call for greater immediate and personal influence of the teachers over the pupils than has been the case heretofore. The difficulties in the way of exerting such influence, except in some general manner, we are well aware of. They are found on the students' side as well as on that of their instructors. But, with a considerable enlargement of the number of instructors, and with constant attention to the matter, much can doubtless be accomplished. The effect of such personal association and influence must, of necessity, be for the exciting of interest in the studies of the college course. Beyond the demands of the recitation-room and the authority of the government of the institution, a power will come upon the student's mind from an enthusiastic teacher whom the student has learned to know as a friend. And thus, in its bearing upon this point, the change which we suggest becomes closely connected with, and almost involves in itself, a change in the method of instruction.

While we have spoken with favor of the compulsory system, as known at present in our colleges, and of the custom of marking the student for his recitations, at least so far as its essential features are concerned, we think that both of these may be modified in the future to some extent. It may be, and doubtless is, the fact, as things now are, that the student is followed too sharply by small rules, and that he is watched at every step too much like a young school-boy. There is, to say the least, a danger under the present system, that many college officers will treat their pupils in a way not only to quench enthusiasm for study, but also to awaken an evil disposition and a readiness to take every unfair advantage of the governing powers. If the matter of excuses is pressed into too great minuteness, and beyond bounds, the result may be something worse than irregularity of attendance. Marks, too, under some circumstances, may become anything but an incitement to real scholarship. It will, very probably, be a serious question with the officers of our collegiate institutions, at no distant day, whether the rules may not be somewhat diminished in their number and relaxed in their all-penetrating strictness; and it is certainly deserving of careful consideration, whether some other method of determining the relative rank of students may not be adopted, which, while accomplishing the same substantial end which the system of marks now accomplishes, will be less likely to repress enthusiasm or to make the daily study appear but a daily task.

The suggestions which we have thus briefly made are only a portion of those which might be offered. But, since they are all, more or less immediately, connected with the question as to the means of inspiring the students with the love of their work, they fall together, naturally, into one class; and since, as a class, they may be regarded as representing all other suggestions of different orders, which might be brought forward, we content ourselves with presenting them alone at this time. To the effecting of these objects, in the way of advancing the scholarship of the college, an increase of endowments will be needed. The Academical Department has great necessities, in this respect, as well as the other Departments. It has, however, a very large company of its own graduates to whom it can appeal for aid. The change in the governing Board of the University, which has been so earnestly demanded by many, especially among the younger Alumni, seems now about to be accomplished. As the want of this change has been claimed to be the reason why larger and more frequent gifts have not been offered by the graduates to the college recently, we suppose we may now be justified in expecting from all, who have been withholding their means for this reason, a large endowment at an early day. Certainly, if this expectation turns out to be groundless, the claim will prove to have been made upon a false basis. But the question will arise as to the method in which gifts from the Alumni of the College can be best obtained. From those of very large property, we should say, it should be sought in the same way as from others of a similar class who are not graduates. There are, however, a great number of the Alumni—indeed, the great majority of them—who are not wealthy. For these the system which has been adopted in one or two other institutions is, doubtless, the best one—namely, the system of contributions by the several classes. If some individual in each of the classes, which have graduated during the last forty years,—some one who is inspired by a warm affection for the College, and who is possessed of some pecuniary ability,—will undertake the work among his own classmates, and will, by his example and exhortations, incite them to give larger or smaller sums according to their means, a very considerable fund may, with little difficulty, be obtained. We know of no time better than the present—when a new epoch of the College history is just beginning and all is hopeful—for the inauguration of such a movement. There is no reason, so far as we can see, why such contributions from the various classes—through the gifts of small sums, from year to year, by the individual members—might not become a constant source of income to the Academical Department. No general movement upon the Alumni, or among the Alumni, has, as yet, been made in this matter of raising endowments. We believe that such a movement, if entered upon now, would be very generally approved, and that the results of it would be surprisingly great.

But for this Department, as well as for the others of which we have previously spoken, a large plan ought to be devised by the governing powers, and, under the guidance of the presiding officer of the University, all those interested in the management of the Department should devote themselves earnestly to the work. With a determined energy and a strong hopefulness on the part of the persons here who are entrusted with the care of the institution, we have great confidence that the efforts of the future will be crowned with success.

Of the other undergraduate department of the University, which forms a portion of the Scientific School, less need be said. By reason of its connection with the professional part of the same school, we have had occasion, in our last Article, to mention some of its wants. They are large, in a pecuniary point of view; but, with the energy now displayed by the managers of that department, we may look for an early supply of these wants. The progress of this school has been one of the most marked things in the recent history of the University, and the more the numbers of students have increased and the design of the course of study has been understood, the more, we believe, has the public favor rested upon it. The question of the future, with regard to this Department, may not improbably be, whether it should not be ranged with the Academical Department as a coördinate preparatory school, educating students for the school of philosophy and the higher studies in Natural Science. But we do not regard it as possible that the two will ever be merged in one, or that the system which has been adopted here, with so universal approbation, will ever be given up for that which is found, so generally, elsewhere. If a University is hereafter to be fully established at Yale, or anywhere else in this country, the result will be, that, sooner or later, the higher schools for professional and general study will take the leading place and constitute the University itself, while the undergraduate departments will be subordinate, and will be for the purpose of fitting young men for the higher positions. But, for a long time to come, these undergraduate departments must be a most essential part of the institution, and must deserve, both by reason of their numbers and their importance, most earnest thought from the friends and officers of the University. For many reasons the Academical Department must, even in the new era of which we speak, continue to be, in a certain sense, a sort of center of the whole institution. But it will be only in a certain sense. The coördination of all the Departments is the work of the years before us. It is the work which will mark the coming time as truly as any of the great works of the past have characterized their epochs. It is a work to which all who have at heart the interests of the University ought to give themselves, according to their position and their opportunities.

The growth of Yale College, during all its past history, has been a peculiar one, as compared with that of some other institutions of the country. It has not been by means of a series of new experiments, or by fundamental changes in its system for the purpose of meeting some passing demand of the age. Such experiments and changes are always attended by great loss of the good belonging to the old things, and they, very frequently, prove to be failures in the end. It can scarcely be otherwise, for the requirements of the agitators or the assailants of the past, who call themselves the representatives of the times, are too generally founded on unwise views. They are the mere notions of men who comprehend little of the lessons of history and as little of the wants of the future. But the progress of this College has been a steady and healthful development. Its guardians have carefully preserved whatever of good has been received from preceding generations, and have, at the same time, not lost sight of the teachings of their own age. The existence of the Scientific School, and especially of its undergraduate department, is one among many proofs of the wisdom of their action in this regard. So soon as the new wants of the country, occasioned by the development of its resources, began to require more thorough education in Natural Science, a school was founded in connection with the College for this purpose. And, again, when the public demands called for a different method, in the more general education, for those who could not pursue the Academical course, provision was made to meet these demands. They were met, too, as we have already seen, with great wisdom, and according to the uniform plan pursued here in the past. Without interfering at all with the arrangements for the old curriculum of study, and by a provision which prevents all possibility that either system should be hindered in its development by the other, the two classes of students are offered their choice between the different lines of instruction, and are carried forward in the one or the other under the highest advantages. The evils of the elective system are thus avoided, while its most important advantages are secured. This is but a single instance of the judicious and healthful progress of which we speak. Other instances might be given in connection with the history of almost every branch of the University. In the Academical Department itself, to which reference has been made more particularly in this Article, the advance has been very great, as those can appreciate who, like ourselves, graduated even so late as twenty-two years ago; and it has been, mainly, with a due regard not only to the past but to the present and the future. With some further changes which the era now beginning will naturally suggest, such as those to which we have referred and others of a similar order in other lines, which might have been mentioned but for the limits of our space, the growth of the Department will meet the reasonable requirements of all enlightened men, without any great revolution and without any severance of the links that bind the College to the times gone by. As one of the most eminent instructors here has recently said, the great thing which we need for the growth and success of the future is confidence in the University on the part of all its friends. There never was an institution of any sort, in any age, which merited such confidence more than Yale College. Let it receive the endowments and the means of accomplishing its ends which it now needs, and all the experience of the past one hundred and seventy years will be contradicted, if it does not make the most wise and satisfactory progress in the period just before us.

There is one subject connected with the whole University, and more particularly, in certain respects, with the undergraduate departments of it, which the length of our Article will only allow us to discuss very briefly, and which yet cannot be passed over without any allusion. We refer to the matter of religious instruction and the religious character of the institution. Much has been said of late on this point, and it is very manifest that, in the minds of some of those who demand changes in the college system here, there is a strong desire for a radical alteration in this respect. In our view, the giving up of the old character of the institution, as an institution whose religious life is always regarded as its highest life, would not only be a change to be most deeply regretted in itself, but would be disastrous to the future growth of the University. The friends of Yale College, on whom it must depend in the future as it has done in the past, are, the great majority of them, Christian men, who believe in Christian education and in no other. Losing the sympathy and support of these men, the college will have nothing to fall back upon. It will sink from its high position, when it thus turns away from its past history, and it ought, thus, to sink. This institution was founded with prayer and consecration to God by the noble men of a past age. They established it as a place of religious teaching and influence, and not merely for the learning belonging to this world. They handed it over to the generations following them, that it might be as a light from God for all time. Every advance, which it has made since their day, has been made by the gifts and efforts of men who had their spirit. It has been as truly a power in the world for the extension of the Christian faith as for the promotion of any science. Its endowments would never have been given to it, but with the implied assurance that it was always to be what it was at first, a religious institution. If by any unfaithfulness of to-day, or of any future time, it should be suffered to pass out of such influence and to take on a new character, it ought to lose its glory and its future. If those who do not believe in religion in colleges wish to establish institutions in accordance with their own views, they have abundant opportunity to do so. But, whoever they may be, do not let them violate the pledges given by the fathers, or lay hands upon a University which owes everything it has and is to Christian men, who have loved it and carried it forward because it was a Christian institution.

To this end of religious instruction and the maintenance of the religious character of the University, it seems to us essential that there should be stated preaching in the college chapel. This service cannot be safely given up in so large an institution, and we see no reason why the undergraduate students, who are, generally, of such an age that, at their own homes, they would be under parental control in this matter, should not be required to attend the College religious exercises. It is to be remembered, however, that, connected with such compulsory attendance, there are some incidental evils, and, so far as may be possible, wise provision should be made to avoid them. For several years past, it has appeared to us undesirable to assign to one preacher the whole charge of the College pulpit. It is doubtful whether any man can accomplish successfully, for any considerable period, such a great and difficult work. If a pastor of the church should be appointed, who should have the general oversight of its interests and should preach one half of the time, and the pulpit should be occupied at other times, according to some regular arrangement, by the rest of the clerical professors or by preachers from abroad, such variety would be given to the services as would make them more interesting and more profitable. It will be a subject of consideration, also, as we cannot doubt, before many years shall have passed, whether the afternoon service may not be, in some degree, changed from what it now is—so that it shall be more exclusively adapted and addressed to the student community, or so that there shall be a more familiar Biblical exercise instead of an ordinary sermon, or so that, while the students are required to attend the college chapel in the morning of each Sunday, they shall only be called upon to be present in some church at the afternoon service, while the choice as to what church they will attend shall be left open to them. We express no opinion here as to the advisableness of any such change, for it would, perhaps, be improper to do so at this early day. But questions in regard to this subject may well be seriously examined when they shall arise, for the determination of the best method of effecting the best spiritual results for the great company of young men assembled in the College may be dependent on the settlement of them. In neither of the undergraduate departments, however, as it seems to us, can the oversight of the Faculty over the students, in this matter of attending public worship, be altogether given up, with safety to the highest well-being of the College. We feel, also, that the chapel, where the religious services of the Sabbath are held, should be designed not merely for the undergraduate students of one department, or even of both departments, but that it should be a University Chapel. It should be large enough to accommodate all the members of the University—not those younger students alone, who are required to attend, but those from the higher and professional schools, who may wish to do so. Such a common center of religious worship might naturally become a means of uniting the whole institution and of making its various members to be one body. To this end there needs to be provided a new and commodious and comfortable chapel, in which the hearer can listen with patience, and the preacher can come into sympathy with his audience and can be both seen and heard. The time is not far distant, we hope, when the present chapel of Yale College will be a thing of memory only. And here we may be permitted to say, that, in our opinion and, we believe, in that of many others, the new chapel of the University, when it is erected, ought to be placed near the center of the college square, and not at one of its corners and the corner of two of the city streets. Its location should be the most retired possible, within the circle of the other buildings, and it should be as central as possible, that it may by its very position, remind every observer that all things in the education here are designed to lead the soul to that which is higher and better.

With these few general and special remarks on this most important subject, which bears particularly upon the academical college and yet has relations to all the other schools, and which, therefore, appropriately follows all else that has been said, we bring our present Article to a close. The Academical Department of this College is strong in the affections of its thousands of graduates. We are sure that it need not fear that it will ever be forgotten, or that its wants, when known, will be long neglected. But the time, we trust, is coming, and the beginning of that time is near at hand in the opening era, when the University, which began with the establishment of this Department, shall have glorified it by taking it up into itself and, thus, making it one of the members of a nobler institution worthy of the future age of the country.

FIFTH ARTICLE.

It has not been our design, in this series of Articles, to discuss all the subjects of interest or importance connected with the future of the College. We have desired only to refer to those points in which the distinctive and peculiar work of the opening era of the history of the institution must most clearly manifest itself. The steady growth of all things, the foundation of which has been wisely laid in the past, will, of course, be cared for by those who are hereafter to be entrusted with the direction of affairs. But this duty belongs to all times—no more to the years just before us than to any other period. It need not, therefore, be urged with any special earnestness now. There are parts of the University, also, of which it will scarcely be necessary to speak at length. The University Library is one of these. Its needs are very great. In its present condition, it is, in almost every section of it, quite inadequate to the requirements of the body of scholars assembled here. Its funds are exceedingly limited in amount—so limited, in fact, that no considerable purchase of books can be made, without going beyond the annual income derived from them. Unless it is much enlarged, at an early day, there is great reason to fear that the whole institution may suffer an injury which can scarcely be over-estimated. The work, therefore, of increasing the Library fund is a work which the new administration cannot neglect with safety. But it is not one of its peculiar duties. The enlargement now demanded is only similar to what has been called for in the past, and will be in the future. The necessity and the obligation are perpetually resting upon the guardians of the College interests. If there be anything in this department, which especially belongs to the coming era, it lies solely in the fact that, as the College is now to be changed into a University, the increase of its endowment, and consequently of its means of usefulness, ought to correspond with such a change. We hope that this great interest—a common interest of all parts of the institution—will, by no means, be forgotten. If the collecting of one or two hundred thousand dollars for this purpose can be made an object of earnest thought and energetic effort, until the end is secured, one of the greatest possible services to the cause of learning here will be rendered. Important as this work is, however, and great as will be the advantages if the result is attained, it will not be necessary to our present line of thought to dwell upon it further in this place.

There are other parts of the University, in which, as they have only just now been founded, the development is so entirely a thing of the future, that it may not yet become those who are not immediately connected with them to urge anything with confidence. Such are the Astronomical Observatory and the School of the Fine Arts. We would only suggest, in respect to the latter of these two, that, in our opinion, it ought to be made to bear in its teachings and influences, as far as by any means may be possible, upon the students of all the other departments. Beyond the special object of educating artists, the mission of such a school in a university, as it seems to us, is to elevate and refine that great company of young men who are to be engaged in the ordinary works of life. Our American education has been too exclusively in the line of the intellectual, and of mere mental discipline. It is in danger of becoming too exclusively practical. We need the power of æsthetic culture to give our students a more well-rounded and perfect mental growth, and to awaken within them purer tastes and nobler aims. By the munificent gift which has established this school in connection with Yale College, the opportunity has been opened for the accomplishment of this end, and we earnestly hope that the officers of all the departments will so coöperate, that the possibilities of the case may be realized. Especially does it seem to us important, that the undergraduate students, whether of the Academical College or of the Scientific School, should receive such instruction from the teachers in Art as we have alluded to. They would, thus, be aroused to greater enthusiasm in all liberal studies, at the very time in their education when they need it, for the more they come to know of the beauty of culture, the more will they be inspired to love and to seek it. The Art School must be, of course, like the other branches of the University, mainly a working school for its own pupils; but it may, in this way, do a great service outside of itself, and the generosity of its founder may be a blessing, in the years to come, to many who do not become immediately connected with it as its members.

But, turning aside from these subjects, we find a great work connected with *the outward life* of the University, which belongs so peculiarly to the coming era, that it cannot be passed over without consideration. The rebuilding of the various College edifices and their entire re-arrangement have only been commenced within the past two years. The plan, therefore, of the whole undertaking and the carrying out of it are left for the new administration. Of the vast importance of this work, both to the beauty and comfort of the buildings and, incidentally, to the intellectual and, even, the moral life of the institution, there can, scarcely, be any doubt in the minds of intelligent men. The plan, so far as it has been determined upon, is, doubtless, the wisest and best one; — namely, the plan which removes the old buildings altogether and, erecting the new edifices around the College square, leaves the interior an open campus. The beauty of this arrangement and open interior will be readily appreciated by any person, who will examine the grounds with this plan in his mind. It can hardly be questioned, we may add, that the main front of the buildings should be towards the interior. This is and must be the fundamental idea in the change which it is proposed to make. The great quadrangle must look inward, not outward, and the College life, so to speak, must find its center within its own borders. But it ought to be remembered, as we think, that the situation of the buildings is quite a peculiar one. They are not at a wide remove from the town, as is the case with many colleges in other parts of the country. Nor do they, as is sometimes the fact, constitute the chief feature of the whole landscape. In such cases, the arrangement best adapted for the institution itself might fitly be the only point of consideration in determining even the minuter details of the plan. They are, on the other hand, in the central part of one of the most beautiful of our American cities. The ground on which they stand, also, is contiguous to and faces the large public square, which is so well-known an ornament of New Haven. Under these circumstances, whatever is done in the matter of locating and erecting the College buildings must have a most important bearing on the appearance of the city. The citizens, no less than the University authorities, therefore, have a deep interest in all new plans, and their feelings deserve respectful attention whenever decisions are to be made. It ought, likewise, to be remembered that a very considerable proportion of the largest benefactors of the University have been residents of New Haven, who have bestowed their gifts upon it partly because it was the College belonging to their own home. As we think of these various points, we cannot but regard it as a thing to be deeply regretted, that the new buildings, which have recently been erected on the College square, have no appearance of a front on the street side. Without interfering at all with the principal idea of the plan—namely, the forming of a quadrangle opening upon the interior—and even without giving a prominent real frontage toward the city, the appearance of such a frontage might have been presented. Instead of turning the back of the buildings so conspicuously and manifestly, as is now the case with the Farnam and Durfee Halls, to the streets and to the "Green," with comparatively slight changes this aspect of things might have been wholly altered. In this way the public square might have been beautified, and compensation made for the loss of the view of the College grounds from without which was rendered necessary by the plan of the quadrangle. It is fortunate that the work has gone no farther, when the new era commences; and we believe we express a very general and wide-spread sentiment, both of the graduates of the College and of the citizens of New Haven, when we say that, as the plan is carried forward towards its completion, all new buildings, which shall hereafter be erected, ought to be designed with this double frontage or with the appearance of a handsome front toward the town. We urge this because it is right, because it is respectful to the citizens, because, while it will be no injury to the College itself, it will tend greatly to the adorning of New Haven, and because the location of the buildings is such as to demand of the authorities of the University what, under a different condition of things, might not be required. Moreover, we believe that a due regard to public sentiment in this matter will meet, in the course of years, a rich reward. The readiness of the residents of the city to give to the College, according as its needs may arise, will be, in some measure, proportioned to the readiness which the College shows to beautify and honor the town where it is placed. If the permanent growth and welfare of the institution are to be secured, New Haven must not fail to cherish and support it. A feeling must be awakened which shall pervade the city, and which shall be stronger as well as more general than has ever been known before,—a feeling of sympathy for and interest in Yale College —a feeling which shall respond gladly to every call, and which shall prompt to generous benefactions on every occasion. This feeling may be awakened. The signs of it are beginning to be manifest already. It, certainly, ought not to be repressed by adopting a course, which naturally may meet the disapprobation of those who feel a pride in the beauty of the city, and which, unquestionably, has occasioned regret in the minds of many most estimable persons.

It seems to us unfortunate, also, that the first of the new buildings, and one which, by its situation, must be very prominent among them, should have been built of brick. The glory of architecture lies in stone, and the cherished hope of those who have looked forward to the coming age of architecture in the College has, we believe, been quite universal, that the old line of unsightly brick buildings might give way, not only to beautiful ones, but to those made of stone. In the case of the Theological Hall there were special and imperative reasons which determined the material. That edifice, also, not standing on the College square, was not of so essential importance to the plan of the future. But, in the Academical Department, the matter is so vital, that it would seem better to make the utmost possible effort than to give up the erection of stone buildings. The small difference in the expense, provided the stone be with the rough edges found in the Durfee Hall, shows that the use of this material is altogether practicable, and the fine appearance of that building must, as it would seem, decide the question in all minds as to the desirableness of using it. We hope that the persons who may have in charge the carrying out of the remainder of the great plan will keep this idea before them.

We speak of the plan as a great one. It is so because it has reference to nothing less than the rebuilding of the whole College. It is so, also, because it must extend over a period of years, and, possibly, beyond the life-time of those who commence the work of accomplishing it. For this reason, it appears to us that it should be *most carefully studied, in all its parts, at the outset.* Nothing should be done as by chance, or without reference to its bearing upon everything else. The committee, which has in charge the erection of one building, should not be different from that which takes the oversight of another. The location of all the edifices, the laying out and grading of the grounds, the general character of the architecture which is proposed, should be determined, so that every part of the plan, whenever it may be realized—whether now or fifty years hence—may naturally adapt itself to every other. The President of the University should possess himself thoroughly of everything which is designed to be done, and should be an energetic power to do all that will help forward the end, as well as to prevent all that can hinder it. No one else can be the center of the University action here, any more than in any other sphere. He is, by virtue of his office, the head and the source of authority. Others may give him the benefit of their counsels and may coöperate with him. But he must be the executive. The responsibility rests upon him and cannot be thrown off. The period of the administration which now begins, or even of that which shall follow it, may not witness the final result, but to this era, which is just before us, belongs the determination of what that result, if ever attained, shall be. If accident or the vain notions of some chance benefactor are suffered to change the plans or to form them, the precious opportunity will be lost. No greater opportunity of this kind has ever been presented in any institution in the country, than the one which is now opened here.

We add, that, in our opinion, the University authorities, with the presiding officer at their head, should make it their earnest endeavor to realize the fulfillment of this plan *within the era of which we speak.* It *may* prove in the end to be impossible to remove all the old College buildings within the lifetime of the present generation, and to replace them by new and more suitable structures. But there is no such impossibility *now manifest* as to make any effort unreasonable. On the other hand, there is more ground to anticipate the accomplishment of the whole work before the next fifteen years shall have passed, if it be earnestly labored for, than there was, fifteen years ago, that a beginning would have already been made. As the wealth of the country rapidly increases, the number of those who make large benefactions to our literary institutions must, undoubtedly, multiply. To such persons the erection of new buildings is a matter of great interest. They are, in general, more easily moved to give for such an object than for any other. With a wise presentation of these wants of the University to men of this class, from time to time, and with corresponding effort to enlist their sympathies, it will not be surprising if the College square shall, at no distant day, have put on a new appearance, and the age of architectural beauty shall, indeed, have begun its progress. It should be remembered, that, in this matter as in some others already referred to in our former Articles, very little earnest effort has, as yet, been made. The guardians of Yale College have never, hitherto, been forward in the work of solicitation. But now is a most favorable time for a change in this regard. Nay, even the very duty which Providence lays upon us, at present, is to prepare for the greater and more glorious possibilities of the future, by gathering the means of accomplishing the results which shall then be opened to view. And, as is very often the case in the Providential dealings—the encouragements are given just as the duty makes itself manifest. Indeed, these encouragements constitute a part of the evidence, that the Divine call is into the line of progress where they lie.

It is the feeling on the part of some, that this matter of rebuilding the College edifices—being a thing of the mere outward life—should be deferred until other and more important ends are realized. We agree with such persons, so far as to hold that the provision of the means of instruction should have the first place in the minds of the University authorities, and that the raising of funds for buildings should be quite subordinate in their estimation. But, in our view, there is no reason why the two things should not be carried forward together. The chief danger of the coming era, which dawns upon us with such great opportunities, is that our plans will not be large enough. They need to be very comprehensive—to have their several parts duly arranged, indeed, and the lower subordinated to the higher, but yet *to include all things the need of which is now manifest.* It is the very law of such enterprises, that the wider they are, and the more boldness and energy they require, the more sure are they to be successful. It will not only require five or ten times as much time to accomplish the parts successively, as to do the whole together, but the chances of failure will be almost equally multiplied. The fearful and unbelieving lose the kingdom here as truly as anywhere. Moreover, as it seems to us, no half-way course is permitted to us now. The wants of the University press upon our attention, at the present time, *not one by one, but all alike.* From every department, they utter their voice loudly, and in the line of outward things as well as of the more inward and intellectual. The College needs new recitation-rooms as truly as it needs new professors. It asks for a new Chapel quite as earnestly as for a new preacher. Let us hear both the calls and endeavor to supply both the demands at the same time. The wants, if they are made known together, will fall favorably upon the ears of different men. The giver who would not care to endow a professorship may gladly build a Chapel, and he who thinks nothing of theological instruction may become to the Scientific School a large and, perhaps, a constant benefactor. How unwise, by pursuing only one of the ends at a time, to lose the opportunity of gaining the one or the other of these gifts, both of which are, as it were, ready to fall into our hands!

But the erection of these new buildings and the re-arrangement of the College square, of which we have spoken, are *not* things belonging *only* to the outward life of the institution. The grand old edifices of Oxford and Cambridge have an elevating power upon the minds and hearts of those who find their homes within them, and it will be so here in the future. The student of other days will not go away from his College life with only those influences which come from the books he has studied, or the minds he has been brought in contact with. The very buildings which have met his vision from day to day, and in which he has passed the happy season of his education, will have taught him other and valued lessons. They will have entered, by their insensible yet constant influence, into his inward life; and who shall say that the builders of them will not have wrought for the welfare of the mind and soul? The accomplishment of the plan which shall effect these results, then, is not a matter of small moment, or a thing not to be labored for at present. The work of the new era, as it builds up the University, should include within itself—even from the outset—this building of a more beautiful home for the University. It should undertake to unite the influences of Architecture with those of Literature and Religion, and to do all things with one comprehensive purpose and by means of one far-reaching and common effort.

The thought which has just been presented leads us to press, once more, the suggestion which was made very briefly in our last Article—namely, that, in the new arrangement of the College buildings, the University Chapel should be placed within the quadrangle, and near the center of it. The strong desire and prayer of most of the friends on whom Yale College rests, is, as we then said, that it may ever continue a Christian institution—a place where religion shall be taught, as well as human learning, and where the science of duty and of God shall be supreme over all others. But, at the same time, there are evident indications that a party is growing up with other views and other designs. It is not unlikely that this party may become stronger in future years, and that a serious conflict of opinion may arise on this subject, the decision of which shall involve vast interests. In view of the possibility of such a conflict, the believers in the Christian faith, and, not only in this, but in Christian education, may well adopt every wise measure for the securing of this University permanently for their cause. Undoubtedly, the end is to be accomplished mainly by intellectual and spiritual means. But these are not all. The minds of men are affected, in no small degree, by what their eyes see. The silent influence of things which strike the senses becomes, in the long progress of time, an effective power to guide and control public sentiment. The location or the architecture of a building may seem a small, or even an insignificant thing, in itself, but it may prove to be of more force than labored argument. It will teach its lessons constantly, and, while it provokes no controversy about the truth, it may bear a perpetual witness to it. In our judgment, the placing of the house of religious worship for the University at the central point of all the other edifices will be one means of defending and preserving the true faith here. To the hundreds and thousands of young men, who shall come to this great institution in the distant future, the turning and pointing of all things will be *visibly* toward religion. The love which the fathers have had for God and his kingdom will impress itself upon every beholder, and their manifest consecration of all learning to Christ and His cause, in this honor given to His house, will be as a continual impulse towards belief and duty. The question now open to those on whom the determination of this matter rests, is not a question of convenience, or of beauty of arrangement, or of the present time, only. It is a question whose decision reaches into the future, and may have a very appreciable and powerful influence upon the moral life of the University in the coming generations. With everything else favoring the location of which we speak—the quietness of retirement from the public thoroughfares, the effectiveness of the buildings as a whole to the eye of the observer, the fitness of the place, if the Chapel is to be, in any way, connected with a memorial of those who died in the struggle for the life of the country, the great appropriateness if at no distant day, as we hope, a chime of bells shall call the College community to worship and to prayer—we would urge, with especial earnestness, upon the new President and his associates in authority the consideration, that, in locating the University Chapel thus, they will be doing a service—how great a one the future only can tell—*to the good cause.* And we ardently hope that, with all which they may accomplish through their direct religious influence and by defense of the truth, they will not suffer the peculiar, though silent, power to which we have referred,—a power which it is in their hands to put into perpetual operation—to be lost in the work of Christian education here.

By reason of the recent action of the Legislature of Connecticut and of the Corporation of the College, the new era, of which we are writing, is made to open with a great change in the governing board of the whole institution. So long as this change was only proposed or desired, it did not fall within the proper scope of these Articles to discuss it. But now that the steps have been taken which render it certain, it suggests some thoughts in regard to the progress and welfare of the University which deserve our consideration. Not only is the work of the coming time a peculiar one, but a new element is to be introduced into that body which must authorize and direct the accomplishment of it. The graduates of the College are to be represented in its administration, and thus, in a certain sense, are to take charge of its interests. We think it fortunate, if this change was to be made at all, that it is made just at this moment. The turning-point of the College history has arrived. Great things present themselves before the vision and the hopes of the friends of the institution. The enthusiasm of the Alumni is to be depended on, in large measure, for the full realization of these things. Great sums of money are required for the supply of wants of various kinds. The plans for the attainment of these ends must soon be laid. It would seem, for every reason, that the time of passing into the new epoch should be the time of introducing the new men. But what may be and ought to be expected from this change? The first thing, as it seems to us, which we have a right to expect is, that the Corporation, both as individuals and as a body, will take a more active part in carrying forward the *outward interests* of the University. The clergymen of Connecticut could not, for obvious reasons, accomplish very much in awakening the enthusiasm of the graduates scattered over the country, or in the work of enlarging the funds. They have managed admirably the endowments which have been received. They have, also, given their moral support to the professors and others who have energetically, and often successfully, presented the cause of the College to the public favor. They have guarded the good name and, best of all, the Christian character of the institution. But there have been regions of effort where they could not well enter. Now, however, influential men from among the Alumni are to take the places of the most inactive part of the body—the State members. They will, doubtless, be representative persons, and, perhaps, from different localities. They will have all the advantage of knowing, by their own experience and observation, what the University needs. They will have, centered in themselves, the personal interest of a great number who have taken part in their election to office. No persons, certainly, can be better qualified than they to do active service in all those ways in which the Trustees of a College can help it forward. They ought, immediately after their entrance upon their duties, to take into most serious consideration the pecuniary wants which make so urgent a demand. They ought to feel that it is their business to aid and to relieve the instructors in this matter. Their office should not be a sinecure. It should not be a sphere for mere giving of advice. Advice from gentlemen living at a distance from the College and its daily life is a thing comparatively little needed. But, if they consent to become Trustees of the institution, they should labor for its welfare. The duty of instruction does not fall to them, but the duty of collecting funds and guarding them—the duty of providing the means of enlarging the usefulness of the University by increasing its endowments—is one which they cannot justly set aside. We do not say that they should do the whole of this work. Doubtless, they cannot accomplish it all. But they should take their share of it, and should feel that it devolves upon them as truly as it can upon any one. And this should be the more deeply impressed upon their minds, because the very reason for this change, which has been urged by those who have favored it, is the fact that such persons could move the graduates and the wealthy men of various places to give to the College, as Connecticut senators and clergymen could not.

We may add, in the second place, that this new portion of the Corporation ought to exert a healthful influence, both within the institution and outside of it, for the growth and progress of the University. This influence can be exerted on the outside public, by instructing the public, at proper times and in suitable ways, as to what the University is and is doing —what it needs and what it can accomplish. They can prevent such impressions from spreading abroad as have been occasioned by the many ignorant newspaper letters and articles of the past eighteen months. They can awaken a right public sentiment, and can bear witness to all their fellow graduates that a good work is going forward here. By these and other means,—the result of wise counsels and warm affection,—they can be of great advantage to the cause of the institution. Within its own walls, also, they may infuse the spirit of enterprise wherever it may be needed. They may bring new impulses from the outer world, and impart something of new life. They may bear encouragement to those who labor in the work of instruction, by showing a readiness to meet all their reasonable demands. They may contribute to the best sentiments and feelings among the community of students, by showing them in how high estimation the most honored of the graduates hold the College studies and life. If they effect these results and adopt this course, the future years will afford great reason for gratitude that this change in the Board of Trustees has been made. But the influence of which we speak must be exerted *in a healthful way*, if it is to be of real value. There must be no restless desire of change for the sake of change; no wild following of the present and passing public thought; no conviction that a university can be made in a day by giving up old rules and old studies; above all, no feeling that power is of no use unless it is continually exercised, or that the interests of the institution and its success depend wholly upon the Board. They must be as ready to be guided as they are to guide, and must be governed by a sincere and controlling desire for the good of the University, no matter how entirely inconsistent the effecting of that good may chance to be with any of their own pre-conceived views. They must be, in a word, a body of wise counselors, who look upon themselves as holding a great public interest in trust.

In the third place, we think that the new element in the Corporation—being composed, as we hope it will be to a considerable extent, of men familiar with business and finance—may be of service in the laying out of wise and large plans. In the single matter of landed property for the purposes of the institution, we hope they may more fully appreciate than some others are apt to do the needs of the future—that the limited area of the College square will be soon insufficient, and that additional ground in the neighborhood should be secured. It requires but little foresight of the future, as it seems to us, to perceive that every lot in the vicinity of the College, which the Corporation now own, must be occupied with buildings hereafter, and that the disposal of any such property to others is little short of madness. In the new era, we trust that no such step will be taken as has been taken, at two or three different times, in the past—when one of the most eligible lots near the College has been offered by the College authorities for sale. This calamity which has been fortunately averted, almost by accident, ought to be guarded against with all diligence in the future. In this and in all similar points, it is earnestly to be desired that the outlook upon the coming time and its wants may be a wide one, and that early provision may be made, wherever it can be, for the supply of those wants when they shall have arisen. We think it may fairly be questioned, also, whether in regard to the investment of funds some changes might not wisely be made under the direction of the Board as newly constituted. No doubt, safety of investment is the chief and all-important thing to be desired with reference to funds held by Trustees for any purpose. Especially is it so, with funds given to educational objects. But, when we consider the low rate of legal interest in the State of Connecticut as compared with what is found in many other States, and when we remember the good securities to be obtained elsewhere—equally good with those which are offered here,—it will scarcely be unpardonable to suggest that *a portion* of the funds might be placed at interest where it could be done with better results of income. The difference between nine or ten per cent and six is a very appreciable difference, and, if it should be made in the income of a tenth or a twentieth part of the University funds, it would do much good. It is true, indeed, that the College authorities have never lost anything which has been intrusted to them. This is much to say. It is even the best of all things for a Board of Trustees to be able to say. But the question, which we think may be worthy of serious reflection and discussion, is, whether they may not, in some degree, change their investments so as to enlarge the annual receipts, and yet, in the future, be able to make the same declaration. The new members of the Board may, perhaps, have some useful suggestions to offer with regard to this point, and may, possibly, add more of wisdom to the body than the Connecticut Senators, whose seats they take, have ever furnished.

The Corporation should, also, keep in mind the idea of the unity and unification of the whole University, in all their actions and plans. To this end, they should not only make a wise and impartial distribution among the several departments, according to their necessities, of whatever funds may be gathered for University purposes, but they should keep all the funds, as it appears to us, under their own control. The creation of separate boards of trustees for the care of moneys devoted to special objects or departments is disintegrating in its tendency. The natural and, almost, necessary influence of it is to cause division. In the course of years, if not at once, there will arise a difference of interests or of views among the boards, and the consequence will, almost inevitably, be an injurious want of harmony in action. One or another of the various bodies will try to gain control beyond its own bounds, by reason of its power over the funds entrusted to it. Such is, to say the least, a *danger* which may befall the institution from this source. The possibility of it ought to be avoided. But whether this be admitted as a thing to be anticipated or not, there can be no doubt that the union of all interests under one government is, in a University as well as everywhere else, the best of all means to the end of harmonious and healthful progress. In an especial degree, may we say, is this true in a University, for, if new boards of trust are created for each new department, it is almost certain that they will generally consist of a few persons from without the institution together with a small part of the faculty of the department. The members from abroad will possess so little knowledge, as compared with their associates from among the instructors, in regard to all the matters appertaining to the institution, that they will, in most cases, be governed altogether by their views, and in this way the control of the funds in question will be, practically, in the hands of two or three professors. If the faculty in general were to be made the guardians and administrators of all the pecuniary interests of the University—if the faculty, thus, were to become the trustees—we do not know that any serious harm would be done. Such an arrangement would be a tolerable one, though, perhaps, not the best. But, in our judgment, there could be devised no more dangerous or undesirable system than that by which the property of the theological or the academical department, for example, should be managed by one-half or one-third of the faculty of either of those departments. There might, indeed, no evil arise from such a state of things within a few years, because the particular professors who should have charge of the trust were honorable men, or because no question of great moment happened to arise which was calculated to awaken selfish interests. But the arrangements of a College are for all time, and the evil will manifest itself sooner or later. The period will arrive when it will be important to use the power, which such trusts give to those who hold them, and when it will be used—it may be to change the character of the institution—it may be to establish the new education in place of the old, or to make the old exclude altogether the new. But—all danger aside—such a system is manifestly unjust, conferring powers upon a portion of a body of instructors, in which others,—their equal associates,—have no share. In the long run, such unfair distribution will diminish or destroy good feeling. The portion who are without control will be grieved and offended, and very properly so, and that harmony which is the first essential of a true University life will be broken up. If we were admitted to a membership in the Board of Trustees of Yale College, we would rather reject a gift of any amount for any purpose than consent, for one moment, to have that gift placed under the control of any other board—and this, not because we should care to have the control of it ourselves, for its own sake, but because we deem it essential to the highest interests of the University. Least of all would we consent to place it in the charge of a portion of the faculty, whether associated or not with other persons. The recent act of the College Corporation, by which they have allowed the establishment of one such Board, is, in our judgment, a very unwise one, and we earnestly hope that the new era may see no further act of the same order. If the present Corporation is not competent to keep and administer the funds, let one be constituted that will be. But do not let us have ten or twenty bodies of trustees governing one institution. Let us be united under one power, or we shall not continue to be bound together as a University except in name. With the change, however, which is now to be made in the Corporation, the charge of incompetence, which some have urged of late,—very unjustly as we think,—passes away. The minds of all complainers are satisfied, and there is no possible ground for the creation of such new boards any longer existing. There is every reason, therefore, why the opening era should find the governing body firm in their purpose in this regard. They should take the ground, as we think, that unity is essential to the University, and that to this unity it is equally essential that there should be but one government, having control over all funds, and extending its sway equally over every branch of every department. We urge this point with the greater emphasis, because, as this is to be an era of large individual gifts, there is a great probability that some persons, in the bestowment of such gifts, may propose to create special trustees. They ought to be met by the uniform and persistent policy of the institution. To such a policy they will, in almost every case, yield with gracefulness, but, if not, it ought to be remembered that present gifts may be gained at too great a sacrifice, and that there are losses and injuries to the life of an institution for which nothing can compensate.

It seems to us, finally, that the Corporation ought to meet more frequently hereafter than they have done. Within the past few years, the institution has very rapidly enlarged itself. It requires, therefore, much more thoughtful care and attention than was formerly the case. A single meeting of the Board, in the hurry and confusion of Commencement week, is no longer sufficient for the discharge of business, much less for that thorough deliberation which is sometimes essential. Indeed, it would appear that no meeting for important work should be held at that time, but that twice a year, at least, the body should be assembled, when they can have a better opportunity to form plans of action and to make wise decisions. It is no doubt true, however, that such a body may come together *too often.* If they meet more frequently than the public business of the University requires, there is a constant danger that they will undertake too much to manage and direct the internal and daily life of the institution, which it belongs to the faculty to control, and which ought to be left wholly to them. It will be an evil day for Yale College—we cannot forbear to say again, what has been said in substance, though in another connection, in our first Article—it will be an evil day for Yale College, if the wise course followed by the Corporation in this regard, in the past, is ever changed. It would be better to have no aid from the governing Board at all, than to have this liberty which has distinguished our institution, and has been so greatly prized here, diminished in the least. It is this which, more than all things else, has made the instructors here so ready to do service to the College, in spite of every discouragement and all insufficiency of support. It is this which has enabled them to accomplish so much, each in his own department, for the advancement of learning and the growth of the University. They have been free and unfettered—therefore Yale College has become what it is.

The election of the members of the Corporation, who are to be chosen by the graduates, will take place, according to the arrangements which have been made, on the day of the next College Commencement. The Board, as newly organized, will, thus, begin its life a few months after the inauguration of the new President. He will have had time to survey the wide field and to mature his views for their consideration, and, thus, will be enabled to coöperate with and to guide them in the best way. With doubts on the part of some, but with hopes on the part of the large majority, these members who come from the graduates will enter upon their work. They may accomplish much for the institution, and the ways in which their work should be done are, as we believe, those or like those that have been now pointed out.

A few years since, one of the prominent graduates of Yale, in reviewing the history of this College as compared with that of another of the New England colleges, said, that, while *man* had made the Presidents of that institution, *God* had made the Presidents of this. Whatever may have been the truth of the former part of this remark, we are sure that no friend of this University will doubt the force and fitness of the latter. There have been three great periods or divisions of the history of the College since the beginning of the present century. The first of these was what we may call a creative period. It was a time when the College, in any high and real sense of that word, was first established. The foundations and plans were then laid, on which all that might be built up in after times must rest. A wide survey of future possibilities and a generous sympathy with all learning were needed in those who were leaders in its work. The most thorough knowledge of men, in order to the selection of wise workers, and the most inspiring enthusiasm to stimulate both teachers and pupils, were especially called for on the part of the one who presided over all. A man of large heart, and far-reaching vision, and great ability to organize and direct, and commanding influence over all men about him, not only in the institution, but in the community and the State, was the man for the crisis. How wonderfully all these qualifications and demands were answered in the distinguished teacher whom the Divine will called to the Presidency, at that time, the unanimous voice of his contemporaries and successors has borne continual testimony, even to our day. The period which followed was of an entirely different character. It was not a time of creating new things and forming wide-reaching plans, but of establishing into a settled and permanent order the things which had been already originated. Traditions were to be fixed. Foundations were to be made secure. The work which had been wisely begun was to be wisely carried forward. The conservative forces were to be peculiarly cared for, and those which had been progressive, in the former generation, were to be made conservative now. Calmness, wise judgment, the slow and steady movement of a quiet mind, the gentleness yet even firmness, which should not only establish present government in the institution, but should be the guide for all future government—these were the qualities that the new presiding officer required for his peculiar work. And where could a man have been found, if searched for over the world, who was more truly after this pattern, than that one who was selected for the important office when the new period dawned upon the College? It was a wisdom beyond that of our human minds, as we who look back over the past cannot help feeling, which summoned him to this post of duty—which made him come forward now in the succession and secure, for all coming time, the good results of the creative era which had just ended. But another and a different epoch was yet to come, and, as he perceived its approach and his own old age advancing, this venerable man, with the wisdom which always distinguished his actions, laid down his office that it might be given to another. The period which now commenced was as unlike, in all its leading characteristics, to that which preceded it, as that, in its turn, had been different from the one which it had followed. The scholarly life of the College was now to be carried forward to a far higher development. Sound learning was to be established here as in its home. Accuracy and thoroughness and breadth and richness were to be made the student's aim in all his work. The love of learning for learning's sake, and the glory and beauty of it as it adorns the cultivated mind, were to become the inspiring power of all within the circle of the institution. A noble example of a Christian scholar, hating all deception and pretence, and elevating before every mind the standard of truthfulness and simplicity in all working,—this was the demand which the times were now to make. As the College was, also, now enlarging itself in its departments towards a future University, this spirit of real scholarship needed to infuse its influence everywhere—that the substance, not the show, of learning might be the basis of all subsequent progress. The twenty-five years which have now come to their close have seen this great end accomplished. The work is done, as we may hope and believe, never to be undone. But who could have been chosen to accomplish it so well as the one who was chosen? No graduate of these many years, since he entered upon his official life, can question for a moment that there was a Divine interposing, at that critical hour, when a new man was needed, and that the guardians of the College were guided as if by an inspiration from above.

But not only may we, thus, trace out the wisdom which has manifested itself in the selection of each individual for his peculiar work—a work for which the others were not remarkably adapted. The fact that each has come in his own order is equally worthy of notice. The men have not only been fitted for the times, but the eras have been in that immediate succession which was best for the welfare and growth of the institution. They have not come in a wrong order. They have not been separated from one another by years of inactivity or of retrogression. They have moved on as by the direction of an intelligent and superintending mind to a predetermined future completeness. The lessons which the past thus teaches may give us confidence and hopefulness for the time to come.

The era upon which we are now about to enter resembles the first of the three already mentioned more than either of the others. It is to be a creative era. As the early beginnings of the previous times were to be fashioned, in the first of these epochs, into a College which should have in itself the seeds and possibilities of indefinite growth, so the various parts are now to be formed into a united whole—the College, as we have so often said, is to be changed into a University composed of coördinate and coëqual branches. The requirements of the new epoch are, therefore, of a similar character to those which were manifested seventy years ago. They are not, however, precisely similar. The presiding officer who now enters upon his career finds everything prepared for his working. The Departments are already in existence, and most of them growing rapidly stronger. The means at command are large, and those which are still necessary may be more easily gained than ever before, because the public generosity is so ready to bestow them. A company of energetic professors, who have already done much for the interests of the institution, are at hand to support and assist him. He is not *alone*, with the necessity laid upon him to *make* all things, even from the foundations. He has only to *unite* and *harmonize* the body now existing in its separate portions—to strengthen whatever is weak and bear forward what is already strong—to bring to completeness that which the past epochs have been gradually building up. The possibility of this completeness is the thing which is now opened. The fourth great step may be taken in these coming years, which shall establish a University in New Haven—a University which has only to develope itself as time passes onward, in order to be whatever the remoter future may ask for. We do not believe that progress is to cease with this period of which we speak. Far from it. But we look upon the century which is now passing and which is divided into these four eras—the three that are past and the one that is beginning—as the period within which the University may be created. The centuries to come will have their work in erecting the superstructure upon this foundation—in enlarging, in ways and degrees beyond our thought perchance, that of which we, in these early days, have made the commencement.

In the course of these Articles we have attempted to set forth the peculiar work of this new era, both in its comprehensive character and in its separate parts. If we have been successful in our undertaking, we have shown what the opportunity is, that is offered to us,—what the extent of the plans ought to be, if the desired end is to be attained,—what the spirit and energy are, which are called for in the guiding and controlling power of the University. The age is to be one of heroic earnestness, if it is to prove the natural successor of those which have preceded it. The heroic element is essential, therefore, to the leader who is to act in it. He needs to have an all-comprehending mind and purpose, as he looks out upon the future—an all-sympathizing and generous heart, as he meets every fellow-laborer in every department of the great institution over which he is called to preside—an all-conquering and never ceasing energy for the fulfillment of the work to which he is summoned. As the choice has fallen upon one who has long been in the service of the College and whose mind is awake to the excellence of all science—as it has fallen, also, upon one who has been held in honor by his pupils and whose friendship is prized most highly by them,—all the graduates, we are sure, will unite sincerely in the prayer that he may show, in his new station, the heroic energy and the large-minded wisdom of which we have spoken. They will hope that, as he goes onward, he may enter, more and more fully, into the fellowship of those who have preceded him as the leaders in the past epochs, and that, by the completion of what could not be accomplished in their days—the final and full establishment of a harmonious, well-developed University here—he may give occasion, once more, for recognizing gratefully the Divine wisdom in making the Presidents of Yale.

www.ingramcontent.com/pod-product-compliance
Lightning Source LLC
LaVergne TN
LVHW021430110826
845150LV00007B/2161

* 9 7 8 1 4 2 5 5 0 7 0 8 4 *